AMAZING STORIES
FROM TIMES PAST

AMAZING STORIES FROM TIMES PAST

DEVOTIONS FOR CHILDREN AND FAMILIES

CHRISTINE FARENHORST

ILLUSTRATED BY STEVEN MITCHELL

P&R
PUBLISHING
P.O. BOX 817 • PHILLIPSBURG • NEW JERSEY 08865-0817

Scripture quotations are from The Holy Bible, English Standard Version, copyright © 2001 by Crossway Bibles, a division of Good News Publishers. Used by permission. All rights reserved.
Italics within Scripture quotations indicate emphasis added.

Page design and typesetting by Dawn Premako

Printed in the United States of America

Library of Congress Cataloging-in-Publication Data

Farenhorst, Christine, 1948–
    Amazing stories from times past : devotions for children and families / Christine Farenhorst ; illustrated by Steven Mitchell.
        p. cm.
    Includes bibliographical references.
    ISBN 0-87552-823-6 (paper)
        1. Devotional literature. 2. Christian children—Religious life. 3. Family—Religious life. I. Mitchell, Steven. II. Title.

BV4832.3.F36 2005
242'.62—dc22
                                                                          2005047677

To my son, Christopher Dirk,
who might aptly have been named
Barnabas,
"son of encouragement."

CONTENTS

1

POPOV'S PATIENCE

On July 24, 1948, very early in the morning, three men came to the home of Haralan Popov. They searched his entire house, turning everything upside down as they pulled private belongings out of drawers and closets. With zeal akin to vandalism they knocked books and knickknacks off shelves. Haralan, his wife Ruth, and their nine-year-old daughter Rhoda watched the intruders fearfully. For three hours these men ransacked the place before taking Haralan along for questioning at the police station. He kissed his wife goodbye and hugged his small daughter. Then for one brief agonizing moment he gazed at the humped-up form of his infant son Paul in the crib. The boy had slept through the entire ordeal. Haralan would not see his family again for more than thirteen years.

Haralan Popov was the pastor of a Protestant church in Bulgaria. Faithfully traveling as an evangelist to mountain towns and villages to proclaim God's Word, he had not always been a Christian. Born in 1907 and raised on a farm in the little town of Krasno Gradiste, his childhood had been one of poverty and hard work. It had made him tough and skeptical. He had no use for God and, as an eighteen-year-old

> *Count it all joy, my brothers, when you meet trials of various kinds, for you know that the testing of your faith produces steadfastness. James 1:2–3*

teenager, Haralan left home to look for his fortune in the larger city of Ruse.

In 1925 it wasn't easy to find a job in Ruse. Many people were unemployed. But, providentially, Haralan bumped into Christo, a former neighbor and a Christian, who invited Haralan to stay with him. Christo didn't have much room. He lived in a tiny apartment all of six feet long by six feet wide. Although Haralan landed the occasional part-time job, he did not earn enough on which to live and the kindly Christo continued to share both his food and lodging. One evening Christo asked him to attend church services. As Christo had been very helpful, Haralan reluctantly agreed. At the church he was pleasantly surprised to find that the service was conducted in the Bulgarian language instead of the old Slavic tongue that many could not understand anymore. He was also very much moved by the enthusiastic hymn-singing of the congregation to the beautiful melodies of Bach, Mendelssohn, and Beethoven. He had always supposed that religion was for the old and feeble-minded, and so he listened with increasing astonishment to a fervent and well-spoken sermon. After the service several people spoke to him and Haralan was in a quandary. Had he been wrong his whole life or were these intelligent, caring people simply misguided? Later Christo invited the pastor to visit them in their small room. The pastor read the Bible and explained the gospel to Haralan. Scales fell, as it were, from his eyes and the Holy Spirit moved him to a rebirth—a rebirth that left him joyful and full of desire to share his newfound faith in Christ.

Early in 1929, when Haralan was twenty-two years old, he left Bulgaria to prepare for a life of Christian service. He attended Bible institutes in both Poland and England. The Lord increased his knowledge and also gave him a helpmeet who bore the appropriate name of Ruth. They married in 1937. A Swedish native, Ruth was moved to say when Haralan asked her to marry and accompany him to his native Bulgaria, "Haralan, wherever you go, I go also."

The years that followed were a blessing for Haralan and Ruth as well as for Bulgaria. Haralan had the freedom to preach and evangelize across the land. During the Second World War, however, preaching became dangerous, and after the war it became twice as dangerous. Hard on the heels of the German Nazis, the Communists took over. Religious freedom became a thing of the past. Puppet pastors were trained, pastors who preached communism instead of Christ crucified. Those who refused to preach communism were slandered, arrested, and replaced. Haralan Popov was one such pastor who refused. So his arrest in the early morning hours of July 1948 came as no surprise to him, no surprise at all.

From his home, Haralan was taken to the secret police headquarters. For the next five months these headquarters became his home. At night he was taken from his cell to an interrogation chamber and was forced to stand facing a wall. Behind him interrogators continually asked him to deny his faith. He had to stand stock-still. If he so much as blinked an eye, he was beaten. During the day he was prevented from sleeping and was put on a starvation diet. After ten days of beatings, Haralan, upon passing a window, saw his image reflected. He later wrote that he saw "a horrible, emaciated figure, legs swollen, eyes like empty holes in the head, with a long beard covered with dried blood from cracked and bleeding lips. In that moment of total, crushing hopelessness I heard a voice as clear and distinct as any voice I have ever heard in my life. It said, 'I will never leave you nor forsake you.' The presence of God filled the punishment cell and enveloped me in a divine warmth, infusing strength into the shell that was my body."*

There is a great sadness about being imprisoned, about being closed away from the rest of the world. A sham trial sentenced Haralan to fifteen years even though he had done nothing wrong. The prospect of being shut up for such a long period of time was devastating. Haralan longed to be back with his family even as he also longed to be back in his pulpit, preaching the gospel of Jesus Christ. He often wondered why God had permitted such terrible things to take place in his life. But the longer Haralan was in prison, the more he began to understand that suffering is to be regarded as something of great value; that it was a fire that would purify him. Haralan's understanding about suffering did not come to him suddenly, but only after much thinking. He remembered verses like "Blessed are those who are persecuted for righteousness' sake, for theirs is the kingdom of heaven" (Matt. 5:10), and "If anyone suffers as a Christian, let him not be ashamed, but let him glorify God in this matter" (1 Peter 4:16). Yes, over time, Haralan began to see very clearly that God had placed him in prison for a reason.

*Haralan Popov, *Tortured for His* Faith (Grand Rapids: Zondervan, 1970), 33.

FOOD FOR THOUGHT

1. What were the means God used for Haralan's conversion? How is it a Christian's responsibility to make these means available to those he or she meets?
2. What have been some difficult situation(s) in your life that God used to encourage you to think about Him? How did it make you develop patience?

2

POPOV'S PURPOSE

It became increasingly clear to Haralan that he had been put into prison to minister to others. His congregation was a motley assortment of fellow-men. Some of them were gentle, others were rough and ungodly, but all were starving physically and emotionally from lack of food and love.

That prison was to be Haralan's pulpit became apparent during his first year of imprisonment. One day a young man named Mitko was brought into Haralan's cell. He was frightened and kept repeating, as he paced the cell floor, "I'm innocent. I'm innocent." He praised Lenin and communism loudly, hoping that the guards would hear him and testify to his good behavior. Haralan spoke to Mitko of Christ as the hope of salvation. The first weeks Mitko paid no attention, but later, distressed and weary, he stopped his nervous pacing and began to listen. Haralan rejoiced. He knew that this was not his work but the Spirit's. In due time Mitko requested that they pray together and so deeply professed his faith in Christ that he wept. Not too many days after this profession, a guard came for Mitko saying that the young man had been exonerated. Mitko left, release papers in his hands, but not before he passionately said, "Pastor, here in this cell I have been found by God because of you, and I shall follow Him all the days of my life."

Haralan Popov had memorized much of the Bible and became known as the "walking New Testament." Ministering to fellow prisoners was dangerous work, and it was punishable by beatings and starvation. There were always informers. After considering the possibility, however, Haralan decided not to worry. After all, informers needed to hear the gospel preached also. He was called to the warden's office many times and told, "Popov, we know that you hold secret religious meetings in your cell! We know you do. When will you ever learn?" Then he would be taken to a special punishment cell for a week of water only. On one occasion, after a week of such punishment, the prison director called him back to his office and said, "What is it with you, Popov? Do you enjoy punishment? This is the sixteenth time you've been in that cell." Popov answered, "You cannot stop a bird from singing nor a fish from swimming. It is natural. I am a pastor. My entire life is given to bringing men to God. Whatever you do to me, I cannot stop doing what my God has given me to do." Consequently, Popov was taken back to the special punishment cell for another week.

But even the punishment cells became pulpits for Popov. These cells were a row of solitary confinement cells, one next to another. A prison telegraph system had been devised. One tap on the wall stood for the letter A, two taps stood for the letter B, and so on. Using his drinking cup, Popov began a ministry. There was no hurry. He was usually there for days on end and his neighbors on both sides of his cell were there for long periods of time also. "What is your name?" he would tap, and after a brief introduction with a bit of general information, Popov would ask his cell neighbor, "Are you a believer in Christ?" Then he would, in the remain-

I want you to know, brothers, that what has happened to me has really served to advance the gospel, so that it has become known throughout the whole imperial guard and to all the rest that my imprisonment is for Christ. And most of the brothers, having become confident in the Lord by my imprisonment, are much more bold to speak the word without fear. Philippians 1:12–14

ing time, tap out to his neighbor the message of hope and love in Christ Jesus.

It seemed to Haralan that whenever he had done his best with one prison group, that the Lord would transfer him to another prison to begin a new congregation. Stara Zagora was one of the last prisons to which he was transferred. It held many young prisoners who were under constant surveillance. During the ninety-minute exercise period allotted to them outside each day, Haralan began to teach these young men English. It was a language they were all most eager to learn. When they understood enough English to comprehend whole sentences, he began to preach the Word of God. Their hunger to learn English brought the young prisoners back every exercise period and the Spirit moved many of them to believe. A significant change took place in Stara Zagora. Many prisoners stopped smoking; cursing was not heard anymore; and a spirit of brotherhood became apparent. Graduates of Popov's English class began conducting their own classes. The Word of God spread.

Haralan Popov was released from prison in 1961. Because his wife had been born in Sweden, she had been allowed to leave Bulgaria for her native country during

Haralan's imprisonment. She and the children had been safe while he was gone. Haralan himself, after a certain period of time, was also allowed to leave Bulgaria. In the free world he continued to preach the gospel of salvation through faith in Jesus Christ. His message from the underground church to the free Christian world was, and is, "Pray for those who are in chains for Christ. Do not forget them. Try to supply them with Bibles, for they will use them for Christ."

On November 19, 1989, the Marxist dictator of Bulgaria, Tidor Zhivkov, resigned. He had held power for thirty-five years, and he was imprisoned when the Bulgarian Parliament voted to revoke the constitutionally guaranteed dominant role of the Communist Party. Today Bulgarian Christians have more freedom than they have had for many years.

FOOD FOR THOUGHT

1. Jesus himself commanded us to think of those who are in prison. (Read Matt. 25:36.) How do you, your church and your family remember the persecuted church? How is this a salvation matter?
2. Why do you think that many prisoners found comfort in Christ?

3

HEALTHY, WEALTHY, AND FOOLISH

It is a wonderful thing to have enough to eat, to have a roof over one's head, and to be in good health. This is a gift of God. Sometimes this gift, however, becomes entangled with self-deception and with greed. Dietrich Bonhoeffer, a theologian who lived during the first half of the twentieth century, said, "Earthly goods are given to be used, not to be collected. . . . Hoarding is idolatry."

There is a story of a man who became so disillusioned with his fellow men that he was not able to enjoy the life God had given him. Born in Austria, Paul Wuketsewitz had a good job in Vienna as a public works man. Actually, to put it more bluntly, he worked for the city sewer system. But there was no shame in that. The job provided him with a steady, decent wage—something to be appreciated during the 1920s when many people were without work. Unfortunately, when his parents died, others in the family cheated Paul out of his inheritance. Bitter and resentful, he became easy prey for the sweet-talking of an immigration propagandist who was trying to enlist people to come and

> *Everyone also to whom God has given wealth and possessions and power to enjoy them, and to accept his lot and rejoice in his toil—this is the gift of God. Ecclesiastes 5:19*

settle in Canada. Packing up his belongings, Paul turned his back on Austria, boarded a ship, and arrived in Saskatchewan in the late twenties.

A farmer hired the wiry Austrian. Paul proved to be a hard worker. Not knowing too much about banking, he asked the farmer to take care of his wages. The farmer, an honest man, did bank Paul's wages, but when the Great Depression hit in the early thirties both the farmer and Paul lost all their savings. The bitter root of anger, begun in Austria, grew larger in Paul's heart, especially after a girl he was dating dropped him to go with someone else.

Paul Wuketsewitz finally settled in Petersfield, Manitoba, about sixty miles north of Winnipeg. He lived as a subsistence farmer and although he owned a team of horses and a wagon, people saw him driving around the countryside on an old bicycle whose tires were filled with twine instead of air. On this bicycle he rode the eleven miles to the nearest store, in winter as well as in summer. Not talkative by nature, he was unfriendly with most who troubled to speak with him. Unwanted visitors left quickly when he threatened them with his pitchfork.

In 1960, the small house that Paul had built for himself burned down. Becoming even more reclusive, Paul now built an underground shelter for himself and his two horses. The shelter was under the manure pile and was quite deep in order to accommodate the two work horses. It also proved to be warm in the winter, as the manure provided excellent insulation. A drum and a pipe were put through the top for air, and Paul, who had by then been renamed by the surrounding people as Paul Bog, slept on straw next to his animals. He had numerous cats, but was on speaking terms with only one of his neighbors.

Twenty years later, the underground shelter burned as well. At this time, Paul moved into a corner of his neighbor's barn. Before settling in, however, he first asked his neighbor to go with him to the burned-down shelter. Together they dug up several garbage bags full of money. Paul took these back to the barn, his new home, and carefully cleaned off and dried out all the money. It amounted to $34,000. Some of the money was very old. Paul Wuksewitz, or Bog, had kept it a long time without using it. The neighbor urged him to deposit the money in a bank and Paul finally agreed. He went, although reluctantly, and handed all his money over to a teller, a handful at a time, knowing exactly how much he had.

Paul never spent any of his money, except on bare necessities. He wore the same clothes day after day. He did buy socks from time to time and when he died he had eight pairs on with the bottom worn out of the first seven pairs.

Paul lived in his neighbor's barn for six winters. Every summer he was back in another manure pile with his cats. (His horses had died and he had eaten them.) When Paul began to stop eating, the neighbor asked a nurse to come and check him. She found Paul quite ill. An ambulance was called and Paul Bog was taken to the hospital. When the neighbor came to visit him later that day, Paul took his hand and clung to it. Pulling the man down, he kissed his neighbor on the cheek. Then Paul died. Naked he had come from his mother's womb and naked he would return.

Paul Bog's money went to distant relatives in Austria. It had been "wealth hoarded to the harm of its owner" (Eccl. 5:13).

FOOD FOR THOUGHT

1. How would you define "miserly"? Why would you agree or disagree with the quote given at the beginning of the story, "Hoarding is idolatry"? What is the difference between saving and hoarding?
2. A man named Roger L'Estrange said: "He who serves God for money will serve the devil for better wages." What did he mean?

4

I HAVE GIVEN YOU
THE ACORN

Many years ago, before television, children used to relish doing a number of things mostly forgotten today. Dutch kids, in particular, gloried in a hobby of sorts in which they imitated Chip 'n Dale. It was called acorn gathering. In the fall, the time when acorns ripened, they would get together before and after school, with pails, bags, and hefty sticks. Into the forest they would march to look for both green and brown acorns. They weren't in it for the money. (A large bag of acorns usually sold for only a few pennies to farmers for pig food.) No, they did it for the fun they had in shaking acorns down from trees; for the satisfaction they felt in fingering the unique shapes; and for the competition in vying for the largest number gathered.

During the First World War, when food became scarce in Europe, the true food value of acorns was brought to the fore. A newspaper article in 1915 reported that fresh acorns contained protein, fat, and starch. Germany began buying Dutch acorns. A Dutch newspaper article of the same year informed readers that acorns "cover the ground like gold and

So God created man in his own image, in the image of God he created him; male and female he created them. And God blessed them. And God said to them, "Be fruitful and multiply and fill the earth and subdue it and have dominion over the fish of the sea and over the birds of the heavens and over every living thing that moves on the earth." And God said, "Behold, I have given you every plant yielding seed that is on the face of all the earth, and every tree with seed in its fruit. You shall have them for food. And to every beast of the earth and to every bird of the heavens and to everything that creeps on the earth, everything that has the breath of life, I have given every green plant for food." And it was so. And God saw everything that he had made, and behold, it was very good. And there was evening and there was morning, the sixth day. Genesis 1:27–31

like gold is their worth. Prices of acorns are rising every day. One buyer outbids the other. Competition is fierce. Families, and not just those on welfare, go out gathering acorns to earn some extra money. This means that Johnny can have those new shoes; that Jane can have a warm scarf; and that baby can have a new blanket." By the end of the First World War, acorns were selling at seven cents a pound.

The truth is that acorns go back much farther than the twentieth century. American Indians, in the days before Columbus, prepared cakes from crushed acorns. Old men and squaws gathered them faithfully. Extracting the rather bitter center of the acorn, they boiled this in water for several hours. The remaining meal was dried in the sun, after which it was baked over a hot fire. A secondary use of the acorn was the oil extracted from it. In the year 1608 a Virginia colonist wrote home to London, England, "Acornes, being boyled, at last affordes a sweet oyle, that they keepe in Gourdes to annoynt their heades and joynts."

The people of England should not have been unaware of the value of acorns because during the 1300s Chaucer wrote about them, saying that the English upper class truly enjoyed them. "They were wont lyghtly to slaken hir hunger at euene with acorns of okes."

Today acorns are still eaten by many people. In Albania and other parts of the world such as Spain, Portugal, and Italy, they are a staple part of the diet. Acorns are very nutritious and high in fat content. They are capable not only of producing bread but also butter. They can be roasted over fire and eaten like chestnuts. Spain and Portugal export their acorns for high prices. Ground acorns are used as coffee substitutes in some parts of the world. Some people maintain that human beings have eaten far more acorns than wheat throughout the centuries.

Actually the acorn goes back even farther than thirteenth century America and Medieval England. Acorns go back to the very beginning of creation. In the very first chapter of the Bible we read this particular blessing by the Lord God: "And God said, 'Behold, I have given you every plant yielding seed that is on the face of all the earth, and every tree with seed in its fruit. You shall have them for food.'"

The acorn is a seed. A seed can be preserved for many years, after which it can still germinate and grow. Melon seeds, carefully stored, have germinated after thirty years. The seed of the Indian lotus plant can be germinated after being buried for more than a century. God has given seeds life-giving elements which resist spoilage for a long time and which make them a very healthful food for us. All seeds are rich in vitamin B and various other nutrients.

The next time you eat an apple and admire its red beauty, or caress a peach and feel its velvety sheen, or see an oak tree in all its majestic splendor and power, then remember the tiny seeds housed within them. Remember the tiny seeds and praise your Creator God who has given us these things for food; remember that He created the heavens and the earth and all that is in them in a mere six days; and remember that He, the life-giving Spirit, also has the power to raise our dead bodies to life eternal.

FOOD FOR THOUGHT

1. When the devil tempted Jesus to turn stones into bread in the wilderness, Jesus responded by saying, "Man shall not live by bread alone." Describe a person who does live by bread alone.
2. Evolution believes that plant life evolved by chance and that one plant gradually changed into another. Creation believes plant life was created on the third day and that it was created good and perfect. Comment on the line— "An acorn is an acorn is an acorn."

5

OF MAKING MANY BOOKS

The Secret Garden is a popular book. Many people have read it. The author who wrote the book was born in the 1800s. Her name was Frances Hodgson Burnett.

Frances was born in Manchester, England, in 1849. When she was only three years old, her father died and her mother had to run the family furnishing business on her own. Mrs. Hodgson wasn't quite able to manage this and some ten years later had almost no money left to support her five children. Forced to sell the store, she was happy to receive a letter from a brother in America who suggested the whole family pack up and leave England. The Hodgsons scraped together what they had, bought tickets for passage aboard a ship and sailed for America, eventually settling in a tiny cabin near Knoxville.

Frances dearly loved her new surroundings. She walked in the Tennessee woods, daydreaming, thinking, and writing. She had always liked to make up stories. As a matter of fact, her two older brothers often made fun of her many fantasies, calling them "bosh" and laughing

Besides being wise, the Preacher also taught the people knowledge, weighing and studying and arranging many proverbs with great care. The Preacher sought to find words of delight, and uprightly he wrote words of truth. The words of the wise are like goads, and like nails firmly fixed are the collected sayings; they are given by one Shepherd. My son, beware of anything beyond these. Of making many books there is no end, and much study is a weariness of the flesh. The end of the matter; all has been heard. Fear God and keep his commandments, for this is the whole duty of man. For God will bring every deed into judgment, with every secret thing, whether good or evil. Ecclesiastes 12:9–14

at her. Offended, she rarely showed others what she had written.

Economically things were not much better for the Hodgsons in America than they had been in England. Veteran Civil War soldiers as well as freed slaves were looking for work and jobs were hard to come by. The Hodgsons barely had enough on which to live.

Frances was a rather ambitious teenager. She thought that perhaps it might help her family if she could sell some of the stories she had written. But she had no decent paper on which to submit these stories to any paper or magazine. So, together with her sisters, she scoured the countryside for wild berries, took them to market and sold them. From this venture she earned just enough money to buy paper as well as stamps with which to mail her manuscripts.

Frances's first story was rejected. Not discouraged, she tried another magazine. This magazine not only accepted her story, but asked for another. She received a sum total of thirty-five dollars for these two stories. She crowed to her brothers and they were impressed. These two initial stories became the first of many and in no time Frances's writing became favorite reading in many magazines. Receiving an average of ten dollars a story, she was soon supporting her entire family and able to move them to larger living conditions.

At an early age Frances married Swan Burnett, a young doctor. They were blessed with two children, but Frances felt that Swan did not make enough money to support the family. It was for this reason that she continued to write "potboilers"—stories somewhat like soap operas that kept readers glued to her words and kept the money coming in. She described her stories in the following manner:

> "Penitent lovers were always forgiven, rash ones were reconciled, wickedness was always punished, offended relatives always relented—particularly rich uncles and fathers—opportune fortunes were left at opportune times. . . ."

Actually, life was (and is) not really like that. But most people like to read that it is—most people seem to have a desire for fairy tale endings. Frances fed that desire and it paid her well.

In real life Frances did not fare as well as her stories. Her oldest son, Lionel, died in his teens. Frances, who was not a Christian, dabbled in spiritualism, the belief that you can communicate with the dead. Besides this she also studied Christian Science. Christian Science teaches that illness can be treated by mental and spiritual means.

Sad to say, Frances passed these false teachings on in some of her books. In two of them children socialize with ghosts. Through these books, Frances was trying to tell her readers that you could remain close to those who died, even as she tried to remain close to her dead child, Lionel. In one of her most popular books, *The Secret Garden,* a book still very much available in local libraries, the worship of nature (pantheism) rather than a worship of God, is put forth.

Frances divorced her doctor husband, remarried, and then divorced again. She was obviously not equipped with the answers needed for a happy and fulfilled life. Living to the age of three score and fourteen, she continued writing while propped up in her bed, to the very end. She died quietly at home in 1924. Her obituary read:

Frances Hodgson Burnett, author,
Died at 74,
Romance in early life,
As a child sold berries to buy
Paper and pencil—won first fame
With book, *That Lass of Lowries*

Ecclesiastes 12:12 tells us that "of making many books there is no end, and much study is a weariness of the flesh." The writer of Ecclesiastes goes on to say what is truly important: "Fear God and keep His commandments, for this is the whole duty of man. For God will bring every deed into judgment, with every secret thing, whether good or evil."

Frances Hodgson Burnett is still remembered by people today for her books, even though she was born about 150 years ago. But in light of Ecclesiastes 12, isn't it better to be remembered by God because His only Son died for you?

FOOD FOR THOUGHT

1. The Bible tells us that every work will be brought into judgment, including every secret thing, whether good or evil. Thinking about your own "work," how does this make you feel and why?

2. How would a Christian define the word famous? If you could write your own obituary, what would you say?

6

DUNCAN'S ENCAMPMENT

Andrew Duncan, a staunch minister of the church in Scotland during the early 1600s, suffered much hardship during his life because of his Protestant faith. In those days the ruler of Scotland insisted on being recognized as the head of the church. Andrew disagreed.

"Christ," he preached, "sitting on the throne at the right hand of God the Father, is the only King and Head of the Church."

For preaching these words, he was first imprisoned for a time at Blackness Castle and afterward banished from Scotland. He and his family were in poor straits.

One day, not too long after his banishment, Pastor Duncan's children cried out to him that they were hungry. How their weeping broke his heart. His wife also, being heavy with child, was very much depressed. Andrew Duncan retired to his study and prayed. His knees scraped the wooden floor and he called out to his God. As he prayed hard and long, his belly rumbled with hunger. In the adjoining room he could hear his children sobbing because hunger was rumbling in their bellies as well. Nevertheless, the prayer comforted him. He left his study with an overwhelming sense of God's presence. He kissed his wife and put the children to bed.

"God will provide," he told them and, stroking their pinched faces, said, "The Lord is our shepherd, we shall not want."

Perhaps the children believed their father and perhaps they did not. The truth was that they were newly moved into a strange neighborhood and knew no one. There was neither friend nor close relative who might drop by with some basket of food. They didn't know anyone whom they might approach for a loaf of bread or a small loan of money. And yet before the morning light shone in through the windows, a man knocked at their door. He carried a large sack in his arms, which he deposited with a cheerful grin at Andrew's feet. Though questioned, he would not say where he came from, and he left without telling the Duncan family where he was going. Upon opening the sack, Andrew Duncan found some money, two loaves of bread, a bag of flour, a bag of barley, and some other provisions. How he smiled and smiled, and smiling he brought the entire sack to his wife, speaking as he did so, "See what a good Master I serve."

The story does not end here. Mrs. Duncan went into premature labor early the next morning. She had not been able to make any preparations as yet for the new baby and panicked at the thought of having the child without a midwife. Andrew did not know whom he could ask for help. They were virtual strangers in a strange land. But again, as on the previous morning, there was a knock on the door. Upon opening it, Andrew found himself face to face with a lady. She had tethered her horse to a nearby tree and had a servant standing nearby.

I sought the LORD, and he answered me and delivered me from all my fears. Those who look to him are radiant, and their faces shall never be ashamed. This poor man cried, and the LORD heard him and saved him out of all his troubles. The angel of the LORD encamps around those who fear him, and delivers them. Psalm 34:4–7

"How is the lady of the house?"

The woman inquired politely and then asked if she might come in to see her. Being allowed to enter, she next turned and instructed her servant to bring in her things and then to go home. Before proceeding into the bedroom where Mrs. Duncan lay, she ordered a good fire to be laid in the hearth. Then, as if she had always lived with the Duncans, she attended the mother-to-be and helped her with the birth. She had linen with her and swaddled the newborn baby in this. She likewise had a box with some medicinal drinks that she fed the mother. Afterwards, seeing mother and child settled comfortably in a warm bedroom, she put five pieces of gold on the table, lest, she said, the family should be in want. Then she left. Andrew watched her mount the horse in wonder, for even as the man on the previous day, she would not tell him her name or where she came from.

Indeed, Andrew Duncan served a faithful Master!

Andrew Duncan very likely remembered his celestial friends and protectors when he wrote his last will and testament. This is what he wrote.

"I set down the declaration of my latter will, concerning these things, which God hath lent me in this world; in manner following—First, as touching myself, body and soul; my soul I

*leave to Christ Jesus, Who gave it, and when it was lost, re-
deemed it, that He may send His holy angels to transport it to
the bosom of Abraham, there to enjoy all happiness and con-
tentment; and as for this frail body, I commend it to the grave,
there to sleep and rest, as in a sweet bed, until the day of
refreshment, when it shall be reunited to the soul, and shall be
set down at the table with the holy patriarchs, prophets, and
apostles; yea, shall be placed on the throne with Christ, and get
the crown of glory on my head. . . ."*

FOOD FOR THOUGHT

1. Every Christian should be encouraged by the reality of
   angels. They are a security by which the Lord surrounds
   His people. Suppose that the man who brought the provisions and the woman who helped Mrs. Duncan were
   not angels. Why would Andrew Duncan still be correct
   in thanking his faithful Master? Can you define faith in
   your own words?
2. In a way, a person's last will and testament is a farewell
   address. What would you include in your last will and
   testament, your farewell address?

7

THE KING WHO DID NOT HEAR THE ROOSTER CROW

Many years ago, in the year 1553 to be exact, a little baby boy was born in the kingdom of Navarre in southwestern France. Jeanne d'Albret, queen of Navarre and mother of the little baby, was very happy. There was nothing unusual about her happiness—many mothers had babies in the year 1553, and a great many of them were delighted to hold a first-born son. But Jeanne d'Albret was not most mothers. In the first place, she looked on her son as a gift from the Lord, and, in the second place, she praised God for the opportunity of being able to raise a covenant child.

Little Prince Henry Bourbon of Navarre learned to pray at the knees of his royal mother, Queen Jeanne. He went regularly to the Huguenot church. (The Protestants in France were called Huguenots.) Playing with other children, he had a rather carefree childhood. Indeed, many things in his small life were good, but there were also some very sad things.

> *Simon Peter said to him, "Lord, where are you going?" Jesus answered him, "Where I am going you cannot follow me now, but you will follow afterward." Peter said to him, "Lord, why can I not follow you now? I will lay down my life for you." Jesus answered, "Will you lay down your life for me? Truly, truly, I say to you, the rooster will not crow till you have denied me three times." John 13:36–38*

When Henry was a sturdy six years old, a secret Huguenot synod (church council) was held in Paris. This synod was violently opposed by the Roman Catholics who hated the Huguenots. Consequently, thousands of Huguenots were persecuted and martyred. Henry's mother wept and the little prince cried with her. They had known and loved many of the people who had been killed. Henry wished with his small but warm heart that all people would love each other and that all people would believe the same thing. But such a wish is not for this earth; such a wish is impossible for this lifetime.

In 1562, when Henry was a strapping nine-year-old boy, the Huguenot Wars began. They began in a little town called Vassy. While worshiping together in a barn, sixty Huguenot men, women, and children were massacred by a group of Catholic soldiers. The Huguenots retaliated and fought back. In the next decade there was much bloodshed on both sides. Henry, although young, was a strong leader and soldier for the Huguenots, but deep within himself he wished for a time of tolerance and peace.

When Henry was nineteen, he agreed to a marriage between himself and a Roman Catholic girl named Marguerite of Valois. Marguerite was the sister of the king of France. Henry felt, and so did others, that a marriage between a prince of the Huguenots and a princess of the Catholics might bring about peace. His mother warned him that this would not happen—that this was totally wrong—but Henry would not listen to her.

Many Huguenots were invited to the royal wedding. August 1572 was a warm month and a fine one for celebrating. Paris was crowded with visitors. Catherine de Medici, the mother of the bride, was happy to see so many guests at her daughter's wedding. This was not because she was a good hostess and trying to mend relations between Huguenots and Catholics, but because she hated the Huguenots with a fearful hatred and had arranged for them to be killed during and after the wedding in a horrible massacre.

God permitted Catherine de Medici's evil plan to succeed. Ten thousand Huguenots died in Paris alone and seventy thousand more were killed throughout the countryside. And a great mourning went up throughout France. Huguenots wept, even as Rachel wept, because their mothers, fathers, and children were not. Henry, the bridegroom wept too, but his tears were tears of fear and submission. When faced with certain death during the massacre of his fellow believers, he denied his Huguenot faith. And the rooster crowed for Henry.

Four years after this massacre, Henry became a Huguenot again. Perhaps his conscience plagued him, or perhaps he remembered what his mother had taught him as a child. Who is to say? Who is to look into another's heart? But it is a fact that some thirteen years later, in 1589, he reverted to Roman Catholicism again when he was offered the crown of France. Lured on by power and by the hope of stopping the continual fighting between the Huguenots and the Roman Catholics, he denied his childhood faith for the second time. "Paris is worth a mass," he mockingly said as he became Henry IV of France. And the rooster crowed for Henry a second time.

As king, it is true, Henry did not forget his Huguenot friends. He gave them the right to establish churches and schools. He gave them a number of cities and jobs. These rights were written in the Edict of Nantes. Henry wanted peace in his kingdom. But did he himself have peace? In 1595 an assassin tried to kill Henry. The dagger in the murderer's hand touched his lips, shocking him. A Huguenot friend warned him, saying: "Sire, you have denied the Lord with your lips and He has touched them with cold steel. If you deny Him with your heart, sooner or later He shall also touch your heart."

Henry's desire for peace, peace on his own terms, that is, never came to pass. The quarreling and fighting between the Huguenots and the Roman Catholics continued. And in the year 1610 the Lord did touch Henry's heart with the steel of a dagger. A Roman Catholic religious fanatic murdered him in cold blood. And so his life on earth ended.

FOOD FOR THOUGHT

1. Is a brief moment of power worth the eternity of God's wrath? The answer to that is fairly simple. But think on your own brief moments of power—moments such as: the short duration of an exciting movie which boosted your adrenalin but which used God's name in vain; the few hours of exhilaration of a soccer, basketball, or baseball tournament which brought you pleasure but which took place during church service hours; or the minutes of gossip in a corridor which brought you a

sense of control but which hurt a fellow human being. Looking up 2 Corinthians 5:10, comment on how your "now" affects your eternity.

2. How might reaction to an illness, a financial setback, or a loss be a rooster crowing?

8

HEARING THE CALL

Edith Cavell was born in 1865 in Swardeston, England. As the blond, fair-skinned baby lay in her mother's arms, contentedly sucking her thumb, no one had any idea that God had chosen Edith for a very special task.

Edith was homeschooled. Her father was a vicar and when he was not in his study writing sermons or out in his parish visiting the sick, he was teaching Edith and his other children. He was an able teacher. Reading, writing, and mathematics as well as foreign languages and Bible study were his forte, whereas Mrs. Cavell, Edith's mother, gave her cooking, housekeeping, and gardening lessons.

Finished with school, Edith became a governess. Serving several families, her last job was in Brussels, Belgium. She very much enjoyed taking care of children. In 1895, because her father had become very ill, Edith traveled back to England. As she lovingly nursed her father, Edith became aware of a calling. She felt that the profession of nursing would be a wonderful task.

So it was that, at the age of thirty, Edith became a nursing recruit. Her days were tough—up at 6:00 a.m. and, although there was some time between the studying and the practical work to eat, her duties were not over until 9:30 p.m. But she survived the rigorous training. She worked hard at her notes, and other nurses as well as doctors saw that she often stood and prayed at the bedside of the patients whom she had helped. One such patient was a young man who had endured an operation, without an anesthetic, for paralysis of the spine. Edith sat with him for thirty-six hours. She also painted an apple-blossom on the fly-leaf of his Bible. Underneath this picture she printed the words, "If thou canst hold thy peace and suffer then shalt thou see without doubt the help of the Lord."

Edith's training period ended. She became a full-fledged nurse, promising, *"I solemnly pledge myself before God and in the presence of this assembly to pass my life in purity and to practice my profession faithfully."* These words comprise the beginning of the Florence Nightingale Pledge, and Edith took them very seriously.

In the year 1907, because of her proficiency in the French language, Edith was asked to become the matron of Belgium's first training hospital for nurses. The school was in Brussels, a city with which Edith was well acquainted, having served there as a governess. Four houses, each attached to the next, made up the entire hospital. For operations, patients were carried down the stairs of one house, into the street, and up the stairs of the next house.

Edith began the Belgian School of Nursing with four student nurses. Her days began early and ended late. She cared deeply for her patients, nursing them physically as well as spiritually. She also loved the girls she was training and often gave lectures informally in the sick rooms. Once a big spider crossed the room as she was lecturing. One of the probationers put out her foot to kill it. Edith stopped her.

> *When he had washed their feet and put on his outer garments and resumed his place, he said to them, "Do you understand what I have done to you? You call me Teacher and Lord, and you are right, for so I am. If I then, your Lord and Teacher, have washed your feet, you also ought to wash one another's feet. For I have given you an example, that you also should do just as I have done to you. Truly, truly, I say to you, a servant is not greater than his master, nor is a messenger greater than the one who sent him. If you know these things, blessed are you if you do them."*
> *John 13:12–17*

"A woman does not take life, she gives it."

The school clinic grew. There were sixty nurses in 1912, and the graduates were known for their gentleness, compassion, and knowledge.

FOOD FOR THOUGHT

1. James 2:18 reads, "But someone will say, 'You have faith, and I have works.' Show me your faith apart from your works, and I will show you my faith by my works." In light of this text, comment on Edith Cavell's lifestyle.
2. What, if any, is the difference between a job and a calling?

9

ANSWERING
THE CALL

In 1914 the First World War broke out. Germany occupied Belgium, and life in Brussels became difficult. Edith Cavell wanted very much to help the war effort. She felt compelled to do her duty both as a Christian and as an English woman. God soon provided ample opportunities for her to become involved. English officers, seeking shelter from the Germans, came to the Brussels clinic. They stayed until their wounds, if they had any, were healed and until a guide could be found who would take them to the neutral country of Holland, directly north of Belgium.

Scenarios such as the following were not uncommon in Edith's day-by-day existence. A patient by the name of "Charlie," an English officer, was awakened in the dead of night by Edith. Seriously ill when he was first brought to the clinic, he was now on the mend. As she nudged the young officer awake, she whispered softly, "Come with me. There's bound to be trouble tonight."

Following Edith, Charlie limped down the stairs. She led him outside to the back of her buildings and helped him

Fight the good fight of the faith. Take hold of the eternal life to which you were called and about which you made the good confession in the presence of many witnesses. I charge you in the presence of God, who gives life to all things, and of Christ Jesus, who in his testimony before Pontius Pilate made the good confession, to keep the commandment unstained and free from reproach until the appearing of our Lord Jesus Christ, which he will display at the proper time—he who is the blessed and only Sovereign, the King of kings and Lord of lords, who alone has immortality, who dwells in unapproachable light, whom no one has ever seen or can see. To him be honor and eternal dominion. Amen. 1 Timothy 6:12–16

climb into a barrel. Settling him in snugly, she covered him over with green apples. Not too long afterwards, German soldiers arrived. They prowled about the clinic, poking into many nooks and crannies with their bayonets, but discovered nothing. Charlie was safe and soon disappeared from the hospital bound for the Axis front.

The German searches of the hospital premises became more frequent, however, as the war went on. Edith knew deep down within herself that her mission to help soldiers could not last. But she would not and could not turn anyone in trouble away.

On August 5, 1915, Edith Cavell was arrested and taken to St. Gilles Prison where she was put into solitary confinement. She stayed there until October, at which time she stood trial. At the trial, she denied nothing and was, consequently, condemned to death. Perhaps the German judges who presided over her trial resented the small woman who was obviously proud of the fact that she had been used by God to help more than two hundred soldiers escape their hands.

Alone in her cell, Edith read. The book of Revelation was especially meaningful to her at this time as well as *The Imitation of Christ* by Thomas á Kempis. In this book she underlined, just before she died, "There is none to help me, none to deliver and save me, but Thou, O Lord God, my Savior, to Whom I commit myself and all that is mine, that Thou mayest keep watch over me, and bring me to life everlasting."

An English chaplain visited Edith the evening before she was to be shot. She shook hands with him, asking him to be seated.

"I have no fear or shrinking," she said. "This time of rest has been a great mercy. This I would say, standing as I do in view of God and eternity, that I realize that patriotism is not enough. I must have no hatred or bitterness toward anyone."

Edith and the chaplain sat down on the edge of her cot. The chair between them served as a communion table. They partook of the Lord's Supper together. Breaking the bread, the chaplain said:

"Take, eat, remember and believe that My body was broken as a complete remission for all your sins."

Edith was deeply moved. Her hand shook as she held the small cup of wine and listened to the words of her Lord and Savior.

"This cup of blessing which we bless was poured out as a complete remission for all your sins."

After a moment of silent prayer, the chaplain began to sing the words of the song, "Abide with Me." Softly at first, but gradually becoming louder, Edith joined him.

Edith had but several hours left, and she used them to write some letters. One was to the girls she had left in charge at the clinic. Admonishing them to keep up the good work, she ended with:

"If any of you has a grievance against me, I beg you to forgive me; I have perhaps been unjust sometimes, but I have loved you much more than you think."

At five o'clock in the morning, Edith rose and dressed. She made her bed and stood by the door, quietly waiting. When the guards came at six, she had just made the notation in her prayer book: "Died at 7 a.m. on October 12, 1915— with love to my mother—E. Cavell."

It was a dreary morning. Dampness filled the air as Edith was escorted, between two guards, into a waiting car. It sped toward Tir National, the Brussels firing range. A Lutheran pastor was permitted to stay with her until the end. He pressed her hand and repeated in English the grace of the Anglican church. Edith said, "Tell my loved ones that my soul, I believe, is safe, and that I am glad to die for my country." After these words the pastor led her to the execution post where her eyes, filled with tears, were lightly bound. One sharp command, and a salvo of shots rang out from eight men. Edith Cavell died instantly, and surely the angels rejoiced, for she was pure of heart and saw God.

FOOD FOR THOUGHT

1. Why was "Edith," meaning "gift," a good name for Edith Cavell? What is meant by the phrase "patriotism is not enough"?
2. Placed in Edith's situation, a month or so prior to death by the firing squad, what would you want to read and why?

10

THE HEAVEN BOOK

In 1981 approximately one million Bibles were smuggled into China by a group of Christians belonging to Open Doors, a non-denominational organization with a number of bases around the world. They packed the Bibles onto a barge that had been especially constructed with the ability to partially submerge itself. The Bibles were wrapped in waterproof plastic and stacked in blocks of forty-eight boxes. Altogether there were 232 tons of Scripture. The project was successful in that all the boxes made it to a beach shore off the southern coast of China. Waiting Christians immediately took more than two-thirds of the Bibles. However, while the last of the boxes were being collected, an army patrol showed up at the beach. They rounded up the people distributing the boxes and seized the remaining cargo. It was later determined that about ninety-eight percent of the Bibles shipped out had actually reached Chinese Christian churches.

In the aftermath of the delivery the government came down hard on some of the local church leaders whom they believed to be involved. One such church leader was a man by the name of Pastor John. Pastor John was seventy-two years old.

Pastor John had ten thousand of the one million Bibles that had been smuggled into China. His role was to store them until he had opportunity to pass them on to other Christians who, in turn, would pass them further on inland. A member of Pastor John's home church informed him that the authorities were coming to search his house. Forewarned that he might lose the "heaven books," he went to a local farmer and together they wrapped up and buried the ten thousand copies of Scripture under his barn.

Several months later, Pastor John was arrested. The government authorities pressured him about the shipment of Bibles they knew had entered China. But Pastor John would not answer their charges. He simply closed his eyes and prayed. His angry investigators decided to torture him. They took him out to the courtyard, tied his hands behind his back, and made him stand on a wooden box about four feet high and less than a foot wide. They placed a noose around his neck and attached the rope to a wooden beam above his head. The moment he swayed, or the moment his legs collapsed under him, he would automatically hang himself.

Two policemen were assigned to watch the condemned man. They sat in front of his wooden box and gambled while he stood there. Pastor John recalled, in those moments of agony, that his Savior had hung on a cross and had also seen gamblers in front of Him. This gave him courage and he began to speak, telling the guards about Jesus. He spoke with conviction of Jesus' life, death, and resurrection. The guards refused to listen.

"Old man," said one of them, "when I reach seventy and look as unhealthy as you, I won't be afraid of death either."

Pastor John stood on the box for days. His body cried out for sleep. His legs cramped, and the only relief he got

Then the king sent, and all the elders of Judah and Jerusalem were gathered to him. And the king went up to the house of the LORD, and with him all the men of Judah and all the inhabitants of Jerusalem and the priests and the prophets, all the people, both small and great. And he read in their hearing all the words of the Book of the Covenant that had been found in the house of the LORD. And the king stood by the pillar and made a covenant before the LORD, to walk after the LORD and to keep his commandments and his testimonies and his statutes with all his heart and all his soul, to perform the words of this covenant that were written in this book. And all the people joined in the covenant. 2 Kings 23:1–3

was when it rained and he caught raindrops on his tongue. An incredible week passed. People came by to see him standing there. It was impossible, they said, to stand so long without food and water and rest. After twelve days, Pastor John was very ill and delirious. On the thirteenth day a thunderstorm erupted. As the rain poured down like hail, Pastor John finally collapsed. And the noose tightened.

Incredible as it may seem, however, Pastor John did not die. When he next opened his eyes, he was lying on the floor. His legs were propped up on a chair, and he had much pain. Someone was giving him water, trying to revive him. In the next few moments, he realized that he was looking into the faces of the two guards who had stood in front of his box.

"Don't die," they said to him. "Don't die, old man!"

"Why?"

It was all his swollen and cracked lips could manage.

"Because He saved you. A bolt of lightning struck the rope above your head as you fell. We know it's no coincidence!"

The guards, consequently, became believers, and as the story spread, many others came to faith. A little later, the prison officials released Pastor John. In 1985, four years after the original Bible project, Pastor John was finally able to dig up his Bibles. The heaven books had been buried for a long time, and their distribution caused great joy.

FOOD FOR THOUGHT

1. America's moral law was founded on the Bible. But in many respects the Bible is being buried today, not under farmers' barns for fear of authorities, but under money, politics, false religions, and other things. A teen in Bagdad, Arizona wrote: *Now I sit me down in school, Where praying is against the rule. For this great nation under God, finds mention of Him very odd.* Why would God be justified in punishing North America? How could His anger be stopped?

2. Is the Bible at your house buried under anything? Is it shared? Explain how and when.

11

THERE IS NO OTHER

God has made a magnificent world. And He has put us in it. From the time of Adam until this present, twenty-first century, we have lived in and have been able to see all the beautiful things that God has put here on this earth. And from the very beginning of time we have had eternity in our hearts. That is to say, among other things, we have a great hunger to know exactly how and why everything in this world works. From the simplest things we see to the most difficult and complex, something inside us wants to know and to understand what life is all about. Something inside us, something God put there, makes us yearn for the everlasting.

This desire for the everlasting, for the eternal, makes different people do different things. Actually, it divides people into two groups.

The first group of people responds to the desire for the eternal by making their own sacred places. There are many so-called sacred places in the world—places people have made into holy places—places where they can give vent to their hunger for the eternal.

The Ganges River in India is one such "holy" place. Hundreds of thousands of Hindu pilgrims come to this northern river to bathe in its waters. They believe that life begins and ends in this water. They believe that this muddy river is holy and that by bathing in it and drinking from it they will wash away their sins and come closer to eternal salvation. They pray to numerous false gods here: gods that they make of silver and gold—gods that cannot move unless they are carried.

The Bo Tree is another "holy" place. It is also in India and is a fig tree. Millions of people have visited and continue to visit this tree. The people who come here are Buddhists who believe the Bo Tree was the tree that Gautama Buddha himself sat under when he became "wise" and "understood" all the things in the world. They present gift offerings under the tree and pour drink offerings on the tree's roots, praying that they themselves will also come to know and understand the eternal mysteries of the world.

Uluru, or Ayers Rock, is a huge rock, five miles in diameter, in Central Australia. The aboriginal people of Australia believe this rock was formed in the very beginning of time and that by virtue of its age it is eternally "sacred" and has great powers. They have performed religious ceremonies on and around the rock for many years and still do so today. In 1985 this rock was given back to the aboriginal people, and it is now a national park.

Itsukushima is a "holy" place in Japan. It is dedicated to a number of gods of sea. Two of these gods are believed to have the crocodile and the shark as their messengers. The people who come to worship here belong to the Shinto religion, and they try to reach eternity by bowing down to nature. They can only reach the shrine at low tide as it is surrounded by water at high tide. As worshipers walk across the mud flat at low tide, they pray to the gods of the ocean to keep them free from storms and tsunamis, the giant waves produced by sea quakes.

I have seen the business that God has given to the children of man to be busy with. He has made everything beautiful in its time. Also, he has put eternity into man's heart, yet so that he cannot find out what God has done from the beginning to the end. Ecclesiastes 3:10–11

All these worshipers of man-made "holy places" belong to the first group of people who do not acknowledge the One Triune God, the Father, Son, and Holy Spirit. They are divided from the second group of people who realize that the desire for eternity is in them because they are made in the image of God. They acknowledge Him as the God who made the heavens and the earth, the God who said, "Remember the former things of old; for I am God, and there is no other; I am God, and there is none like Me" (Isa. 46:9).

This second group of people needs no "holy" earthly place because they themselves are a holy people who worship the one and only God. This group of people is called the church of God or the bride of Christ. The people who belong to this second group realize that they will never be able to understand God's plan from beginning to end, but this doesn't matter to them. They know that God has made them for Himself and this is enough. They know that God has made them to serve Him, that He directs every step of their lives, and that He will, in the end, take them to be with Him forever in eternity where they shall know fully even as they are fully known by Him now.

FOOD FOR THOUGHT

1. After Joshua had led the Israelites into Canaan, he made a strong statement. He said, "If it seems evil to you to serve the Lord, choose for yourselves this day whom you will serve, whether the gods which your fathers served that were on the other side of the River, or the gods of the Amorites, in whose land you dwell. *But as for me and my house, we will serve the Lord.*" How do you know that your house serves God? Why do you agree or disagree that there are only two kinds of people—those who worship God and those who worship something else?

2. Why do you suppose that a football stadium, a brand new car, and the office of the president might be called "holy" places?

12

THE LONDONDERRY DOUGH BOY

In 1327, on the fourth of June, in the first year of the reign of the English King Edward, one John Brid, a baker, was taken to court on the charges of falsehood, malice, and deceit. These were rather heavy charges for a baker! It seems that John Brid had been discovered with a hole in his molding board, his table for kneading. Now a hole in a table is in and of itself no sin. However, when people who baked their bread in his oven (because few people had an oven in those days) brought John Brid their dough, he placed their dough on this particular table. Again, so far no crime. The deceit only began when John Brid contrived the plan to secretly place one of his household members under the table. This person skillfully, bit by bit, pulled down small pieces of other people's dough through the hole and put them into a basket. After the customers used the oven and went home, John Brid brought out the basket of stolen dough. He kept the extra dough. Greed motivated him, and he was not in the "yeast" concerned about "loafing" around with food that was not his own. He gleefully sold it to other customers and pocketed the money.

The hole in his table, however, was discovered one day. Fleeced and angry customers reported John Brid to the bailiff. The bailiff, together with the sergeant-at-arms, for so the police constable was called, checked out John's table and had no trouble locating the deceitful hole. (Or perhaps it is better stated that they found the deceitful man, for a hole in and of itself, as was said before, is neither good nor bad.) The evidence was not in favor of John Brid and on June 4, 1327, the bailiff and the sergeant-at-arms marched him to court.

Although charged with falsehood, malice, and deceit, John Brid stoutly pled not guilty. His word, however, was not good enough, and the testimony of those who had visited his bakery convinced the jurors that John Brid was unequivocally guilty.

But now, what to do with the man? The mayor and the aldermen of London talked together about meting out fair punishment. They concluded that John Brid's crime constituted theft and that because theft was neither right nor pleasing in the sight of God, the punishment should fit the crime.

In the end John Brid was put into a pillory, with a quantity of dough hanging from his neck. There he stood, totally shamed, from early morning until evening vespers, a tangible warning to all bakers who might have entertained similar thoughts.

Perhaps humiliation taught John Brid the valuable lesson that honesty is the best policy; perhaps he became acquainted with the fact that your sin will always find you out; or perhaps, although this is doubtful in view of his smudged reputation, he continued as a hardened dough boy robber.

There are differences between the medieval jury system and our modern one. Whether an act is neither right nor pleasing to God is rarely verbalized in a courtroom anymore. Penalties for failure to maintain sanitary conditions on bak-

> *Unequal weights and unequal measures are both alike an abomination to the LORD. Proverbs 20:10*

ing premises, or for adding forbidden ingredients are usually fines, not the hanging of dough from a corporate president's neck. But where is a man's conscience situated? Is it in his pocketbook or in his heart? And how should one do penance? Should he do it in a private lawyer's office or on public knees?

FOOD FOR THOUGHT

1. Do you think that the punishment meted out to John Brid was fair? Why or why not? Would pillories, if they were used today, be helpful in discouraging dishonesty? Why or why not?
2. Is repentance necessary for a changed life? Can you prove your answer?

13

INDEED, THE VERY HAIRS

During the summer of 2000, the headlines of an Ontario newspaper spelled out in large block letters, ACCIDENTS HAPPEN IN PARADISE TOO. The story that followed these headlines was a very sad one. It concerned two children, both twelve years old.

John Simons and Anne Foster,* both seventh grade students at Graft Township Central Public School in Underword, Ontario, went on an annual, overnight field trip with their teacher, some adult supervisors, and fellow students. Prior to the outing, the entire seventh grade class had been very excited. They were to travel north to Tobermory, a small tourist and fishing town, and from there take a boat trip to Flowerpot Island in the Georgian Bay. The overnight camping on Flowerpot Island was regarded as phenomenal by the whole class. Consequently, there was camaraderie during the bus trip; there were songs, and giggling, and a general spirit of hilarity reigned.

*Actual names of the children and their hometown have been changed.

Are not two sparrows sold for a penny? And not one of them will fall to the ground apart from your Father. But even the hairs of your head are all numbered. Fear not, therefore; you are of more value than many sparrows. Matthew 10:29–31

The school had designed this particular field trip to instill leadership qualities into the seventh grade students and to prepare them for their year in eighth grade. The students were slated to become knowledgeable about camping, to learn about the many shipwrecks buried in Georgian Bay in Fathom Five National Marine Park and to walk about the island while being introduced to some rare plant species.

The bus trip, the boat trip to the island, the nature walks, and the camping all went without a hitch. The Friday morning of the return to the mainland, however, dawned bleak and stormy. The bay was restless and the waves were choppy. Nevertheless, The True North II, a glass-bottomed boat, picked up the high-spirited children to take them back to Tobermory. Some fifteen minutes into their trip, seven-foot waves began to pound the boat and to splash over the railings. As the ever-larger waves crashed in over the edge of the boat, a side door was taken right off its hinges. Suddenly the boat took on a great deal of water, plummeting down into the chilly waters of Georgian Bay within one minute. No one on board was wearing life jackets. Thirteen students and seven adults struggled in the cold water. Eleven students and seven adults made it back to the shore, clinging to the two life rafts that had also been swept overboard. Two students did not make it back to Flowerpot Island.

Funerals were conducted that week—funerals for two children who were only twelve years old. The mystified minister who conducted the funeral for John Simons described the deaths as unfair. He said:

"These two young lives full of potential were just a boy and a girl falling victim to the danger and death that is a central part of life in our world. . . . Their deaths were not a part of divine design but rather a consequence of the separation of humanity from God. . . . It's not supposed to be this way. . . . The world should be a place where kids can be kids and a family which gives much to the community should not have something so great taken away."

There is a Jewish saying, "No man hurts his finger here below, unless it is so disposed for him by God."

There is no quick remedy for the pain and sorrow of losing a child, a friend, and a classmate. We cannot understand the ins and outs of God's reasons for doing things. But we do know that our Father in heaven is omnipotent and omniscient, and that He deeply cares and embraces with great love those who turn to Him. And, for now, that is enough!

FOOD FOR THOUGHT

1. What does it mean that God is omnipotent and omniscient?
2. Deuteronomy 29:29 says: "The secret things belong to the Lord our God, but the things that are revealed belong to us and to our children forever, that we may do all the words of this law." Why was the minister conducting the funeral incorrect in his assumption that John's and Ann's deaths were not a part of divine design?

14

HUMILITY

Augustine once said: "Should you ask me: What is the first thing in religion? I should reply: the first, second and third thing therein is humility."

Aidan (?–651 A.D.) was an Irish Celtic monk and the first Bishop of Lindisfarne. Lindisfarne is an island near the English mainland. Aidan brought fellow workers to this island and founded a school there. In this school he trained English boys for service to God. Aidan's efforts to evangelize the island were supported by his friend, King Oswald of Northumbria. Aidan is said to have been deeply concerned for the poor as well and to have devoted much attention to the ransoming and educating of slaves for the priesthood.

Now a poignant story is recounted of Aidan. He usually traveled on foot, going from place to place, ministering to people and preaching the gospel. King Oswald, who was very fond of Aidan and who believed him to be a man of God, gave him a horse on which to ride. This horse was a fine, muscular creature. It was beautiful and powerful to look upon and well able to carry Aidan across the rivers and rough roads of Lindisfarne, especially in inclement weather. Not long after Oswald gave him the steed, Aidan met a beggar at the roadside. He was a very poor man indeed, who, with hands outstretched, asked the bishop for alms. Aidan felt compassion for the wretch and, jumping off his newly-acquired horse, freely gave it to the man. The beggar, amazed at such a gift, thanked the bishop profusely and rode away praising God. You must note that the horse had royal trappings; that is to say, it was covered with a rich cloth, had silver bells and leather reins as well as a wonderful leather saddle. Surely the beggar had been given a pot of gold!

When the news of Aidan's generosity reached the king, the king was surprised and just a trifle miffed. After all, it had been his horse and he had given it to Aidan, not to some unknown, wretched beggar. Consequently, the next time Aidan dined with his monarch, Oswald asked him directly why he had given away such a useful and very expensive present. Aidan answered without hesitation.

"What are you saying, your majesty? Is this child of a mare more valuable to you than a child of God?"

The king was silent. He got up from his place at the table and walked over to the hearth where a warm fire burned. The glow of the flames shone on his face as he brooded. Suddenly he turned, looked at the bishop and unbuckled his sword. This he handed to a servant. Then, without his sword, he strode over to Aidan, knelt at his feet and begged his forgiveness. It was a very humble act—an act that showed that the king understood that material things are nothing but gifts from our heavenly Father to be used in service to Him.

After this, the king sat down again at the supper table. He ate and drank and spoke cheerfully to Aidan. It is true of Christians that after they deal with a difficult matter, a humiliating matter, but one which God requires of them, that they begin to feel a wellness and wholeness quite unlike anything

> *Have this mind among yourselves, which is yours in Christ Jesus, who, though he was in the form of God, did not count equality with God a thing to be grasped, but made himself nothing, taking the form of a servant, being born in the likeness of men. And being found in human form, he humbled himself by becoming obedient to the point of death, even death on a cross. Philippians 2:5–8*

else. So it was with King Oswald. But Bishop Aidan began to be sad of countenance and was overcome by tears. As he wept the king was puzzled and asked what troubled him. Aidan, however, would not say why he was weeping. But later, in a low voice and in his own language, he spoke to a fellow countryman at his side. It was a language the king and the others present did not understand.

"The reason I cry," Aidan said, "is that I know that King Oswald will not live very long, for I have never before seen a humble king."

It was only a feeling, a foreboding that Aidan had. It is certainly not true that humble people frequently die at an early age. But, sadly enough, history does bear out the fact that Oswald, King of Northumbria, died in the seventh year of his reign in the battle of Maserfield by the hand of the pagan King Penda of Mercia.

This small anecdote certainly does not prove whether or not Aidan and Oswald were true Christians. It simply illustrates a humble act. Because humility is, among other things, a matter of works—of doing. The Son of Man did not come to be served, but to serve (Matt. 20:28).

FOOD FOR THOUGHT

1. Is humility an emotion, an attitude, a decision, or all of these? Can you be an active Christian without humility? Explain your answers.

2. Jonathan Edwards said, "Nothing sets a person so much out of the devil's reach as humility." Why do you agree or disagree with that statement?

15

THE PROFOUND MYSTERY OF GOD'S LOVE

The five children had been tucked into their beds. Evening prayers had been offered by all of them with the exception of the baby in the cradle who sucked contentedly and noisily on a wet thumb.

"Mother," the voice of the oldest child whispered urgently through the candlelight. "Mother, do you suppose Father is getting ready for bed too?"

"I don't know."

The mother's voice was soft and gentle as she kissed each child in turn.

"What do you suppose he is doing then?"

The mother did not immediately answer but sat down on a rocking chair by the window. The stars shone brightly through the glass panes and the moon was a sickle of yellow.

"I'll tell you a story," she said, "a story about your father."

And the child was quiet and listened.

Husbands, love your wives, as Christ loved the church and gave himself up for her, that he might sanctify her, having cleansed her by the washing of water with the word, so that he might present the church to himself in splendor, without spot or wrinkle or any such thing, that she might be holy and without blemish. In the same way husbands should love their wives as their own bodies. He who loves his wife loves himself. Ephesians 5:25–28

"In 1522," she began, folding her hands in her lap as she did so, "some forty-five years ago, your grandmother was out walking in her Belgian village of Bray. When she reached the village square, she stopped to listen to a monk who was preaching—a monk who was not Roman Catholic—a monk who had become Protestant. Many of your grandmother's neighbors were out in the village square as well, and they stood around her. Everyone was curious as to what this man would say. He did not keep them waiting, and your grandmother was so moved by the words of salvation, words which she had never heard from a priest before, that she put her hands on her stomach and prayed. She prayed that the child in her belly would become a preacher too; that the child who was not yet born would be able to speak of God's love and comfort in the same way that this monk had spoken. God answered that prayer, as indeed, He answers all prayer to Him. And do you know how He answered that prayer?"

The oldest child sat up in bed.

"Yes, mother, I know. Father was the baby in her belly, wasn't he? And father became a preacher, didn't he?"

"Yes. You've heard father tell the story many times before, haven't you? But now you must go to sleep. It's very late."

She stood up, kissed the children and blew out the candle.

"I'll be downstairs, little ones."

Only God's candle, the faint light of the moon, remained, and the children blinked sleepily into its steadiness as they drifted off to sleep.

Downstairs Catherine de Bres took a letter out of her apron pocket. It had lain against her heart all the time that she had spoken to the children. It was a letter from her husband, Guido de Bres, presently in jail for his uncompromising preaching of the gospel. She sat down in front of the fireplace and smoothed the white surface of its pages with her hand. How she loved this man whom the Lord had given her! How she had loved to hear him preach both inside churches or, as was more often the case, outside in the fields where thousands of people had gathered to hear him and other pastors proclaim salvation through God's grace alone. This was only the eighth year of their marriage, and it had been a good eight years despite the fact that they had been forced to move several times because of persecution.

"Beloved wife and sister in the Lord Jesus" the letter began. Tears blurred Catherine's vision at the sight of Guido's familiar handwriting, and she had to wipe her eyes before she could read on. *"I go first and, when it pleases God, you shall follow. Rest assured that our parting is not forever. . . . Our earthly home is temporal but heaven is eternal. Therefore, let us long for heaven. I bid you, dearest, to think of the comfort of these things."*

Catherine wiped her eyes again and stroked the paper as she would have stroked her husband's arm. *"Mark the* honor God has bestowed by giving you not only a husband who was a minister of the Word, but also one who was esteemed to such a degree by God that he was counted worthy to wear the martyr's crown. Such an honor even the angels are not given."

The fire crackled in the fireplace and upstairs the baby murmured in sleep. It was peaceful in the living room and Catherine found it difficult to believe that her husband would not return to this home. *"I am imprisoned in the most inaccessible and most unbearable dungeon imaginable. Fresh air comes in only through a small and putrid sewage opening. The irons on my hands and feet are thick and heavy—an unrelenting hell chafing against my poor bones."* Catherine sobbed and gripped the sides of her chair. The letter fell to the floor and she bent over to pick it up.

"Since my imprisonment I have matured and learned more than I have in my whole previous life. It is a good school God has enrolled me in. The Holy Spirit continually sustains and teaches me. Though Satan prowls around like a roaring lion, he cannot frighten me. The Lord's comforting words, "Fear not, for I have overcome the world," make me the victor. I see the Lord crush Satan under my feet and experience His power through my weakness. . . ."

She had always known that it would end this way. Standing up rather unsteadily she walked over to the table and picked up a small booklet that lay there. Turning it over in her hands she held words, sentences, and paragraphs of faith. In her mind's eye she could see her husband bent over his desk, writing, stopping only to eat when she brought him food. He had read small excerpts to her from time to time, and she had been proud to listen. She returned to the chair and began to read the booklet. Her husband's voice echoed from the pages, and the confession of faith that had condemned him to death brought her great comfort. Such was the mystery of God's love.

FOOD FOR THOUGHT

1. From 1515 to 1555, Charles V of Spain ruled the Netherlands, which at that time comprised Holland, Belgium, and Northern France. Charles V, son of Ferdinand and Isabella, ruled with a Catholic fist. He issued many decrees—no discussion of faith, no Protestant literature, no insulting remarks regarding images of God, the virgin Mary, or the saints—and failure to obey these decrees (and many others) resulted in torture and death. His successor, Philip II, was even more strict. Which laws today would parallel those issued by Charles V and Philip II?

2. It was a hard time for godly families, a most uneasy time for mothers in Israel, because to do a husband good, that is to say, to encourage a husband to remain faithful, would often end in death. How would you have encouraged Guido de Bres if he had been your father?

16

LOVE THAT WILL NOT LET GO

In 1561 a number of Protestants publicly sang psalms in the streets of Tournai, a city in Belgium. Although the singing was peaceful, it angered the authorities. Psalm singing had been forbidden. The result of this singing was that many were arrested. Charges of acting unlawfully were laid against them. To gainsay these charges, Guido de Bres, faithful preacher and loving husband and father of a growing family, had written a booklet. The booklet began with a letter to King Philip II and contained a message for the authorities of the Netherlands. Guido wrote that although Protestants were ready to obey the government in all things lawful, they would *"offer their back to stripes, their tongues to knives, their mouths to gags, and their whole bodies to the fire,"* rather than deny the truth written in the Bible. Guido then took a copy of this confession, packaged it neatly and tossed it over the castle wall where the commissioners of Philip the Second's regent were staying.

Shortly afterward Guido was arrested and put in jail. To his mother whose godly prayer for a believing child had

been heard above and far beyond her expectations, Guido
wrote:

*"You prayed that the child you carried might become a
preacher. God has called me to a holy service, not in the doctrine
of men, but to preach the pure and simple Word. Do not let it
grieve you too much then, if God were to take me as a sweet-
smelling sacrifice and if He wants to use my death to strengthen
His people. . . . Farewell, my dear mother. May the Lord comfort
you in this bereavement. May 19, 1567. Your son, who loves you
dearly, Guido de Bres, imprisoned and in chains for Jesus Christ,
the Son of God."*

In the early morning hours of May 31, 1567, De Bres
and De la Grange, a fellow preacher, were informed that
they were going to die at 6 a.m. They were allowed to leave
their cells long enough to bid goodbye to their fellow
prisoners. Guido used this opportunity to speak of the joy
that was his because he would be permitted to die for
Christ. He encouraged the other prisoners to stay firm in
the faith.

"It appears to me," he testified to them, "that my soul
has wings to ascend into heaven, for I have been invited to
the wedding feast of my Lord, the Son of God."

De Bres and De la Grange were taken to the courthouse
to hear their sentences read—"to be hung and strangled."
They were not convicted of false doctrine but of being rebel-
lious even though Guido had always encouraged people to be
subject to the king.

As Guido came to the ladder and the noose was placed
around his neck, he knelt down to pray. It was not permitted. He was roughly pulled up and pushed on. But with
the noose around his neck, he still calmly addressed
the great throng of watching and anxious people in the
city square.

> *For here we have no lasting city, but we seek the city that is to come. Through him then let us continually offer up a sacrifice of praise to God, that is, the fruit of lips that acknowledge his name. Do not neglect to do good and to share what you have, for such sacrifices are pleasing to God. Obey your leaders and submit to them, for they are keeping watch over your souls, as those who will have to give an account. Let them do this with joy and not with groaning, for that would be of no advantage to you. Hebrews 13:14–17*

"Obey . . . pay respect to those in authority over you. . . ."

But the executioner had been signaled not to let him finish. Abruptly the ladder was pulled away from under his feet. Guido de Bres's soul now indeed had wings and ascended to the wedding feast of Christ.

FOOD FOR THOUGHT

1. The Synod of Dordt in 1618 adopted Guido de Bres's booklet, known as the Belgic Confession, as a confession of the Reformed churches. Why do you suppose, after reading Guido's story, this Confession was and is important to you and your family today?
2. The prayer that Guido's mother prayed for a son who would preach salvation came true. Do you suppose that she might have ever regretted her prayer? Why or why not? What sort of things do you pray for to God that will glorify His name?

17

LOVE ONE ANOTHER

You have heard, no doubt, of the great hostilities that used to burn between clans in the highlands of Scotland. A sad matter! Yet I will now tell you a story that took place in these highlands of an honorable man who put the virtue of word and truth before revenge and lying.

In 1550 or thereabouts, the eldest son of a high chief, whose name was Lamond, was out hunting. At the same time the son of an opposing clan's chief by the name of MacGregor was also out hunting. Both lads, in their zeal in pursuing a deer, came perilously close to the boundary line that had been drawn up between their two properties.

An able hunter, young Lamond had shot a beautiful hart with an arrow. Leaping away wounded, the hart had plunged into a river but even in its death throes was able to make its way across the boundary line into MacGregor territory. Young Lamond was hard on its heels. At the same time, and unbeknown to Lamond, young MacGregor had wounded a red deer as well on his own property. These two deer, in their death flight, passed one another, and as they passed, one of them fell down and died. This deer was claimed by both of the youths who, each swift in pursuit of his own quarry, met

For God so loved the world, that he gave his only Son, that whoever believes in him should not perish but have eternal life. For God did not send his Son into the world to condemn the world, but in order that the world might be saved through him. John 3:16–17

at the carcass of this fallen animal. Disputing hotly over who had killed the deer which lay dead before them, the lads began to fight. Unfortunately, young MacGregor was fatally wounded and died there next to the animal.

MacGregor's attendants, who were not long in showing up, pursued Lamond through the brush. He, not familiar with the countryside, ran through MacGregor forest for hours half-crazed with fear and weariness. Providence would have it that he stumbled upon the house of the boy he had just killed, the house of MacGregor of Glenstrae. He threw himself on the old chief's mercy, saying that he had just slain a man in honest combat and that he was being pursued by a band of the slain man's fellows. MacGregor gave Lamond shelter, unaware that he was sheltering his son's killer. When the pursuers arrived not too much later, they told the old chief that his son, his only son, had fallen. MacGregor wept bitterly, but despite the goading and harassment of the lesser chiefs, would not touch the lad he had promised to shelter. He had promised young Lamond protection, and even though he grieved most horribly for his son, he would not break his word. MacGregor's councilors derided the old man, mocking him even as he wept, but he stood firm. Nevertheless, as evening fell, these evil men extracted the promise from old MacGregor that he should allow them to slay young Lamond the next morning. It was only with this promise that their "eye for an eye and a tooth for a tooth" frenzy could be abated for a few hours.

In the small hours of the night, however, old MacGregor, weary with grief and numb of heart, shook young Lamond as he slept next to him.

"Wake up, lad. I'll lead you away from here."

And holding the hand of the one who had robbed him of his son, his only son, MacGregor softly strode past the sleeping men sprawled around the hearth fire. He walked his charge to the shore of Lochfine. Procuring a boat, he made young Lamond board it and ordered the boatmen, who slept by these vessels, to safely conduct the boy across the loch back to his own territory.

"I have now kept my promise," the old man said on parting with Lamond, "and henceforth I am your enemy. Beware of the revenge of a father for his only son!"

Lamond could not answer. He was impressed by both the faithfulness of the old man to his word and the stark grief in the old man's eyes.

Not many years after this, old MacGregor was ousted by the lower chiefs in his clan. Having no young son to defend and stand up for him, he was in the end but an old man, an old and broken widower, with no place to go. Young Lamond, having come into his deceased father's estate and hearing of Laird MacGregor's ill fortune, came and beseeched the old man to take refuge under his roof. The old man went and until he died was treated as a father by Lamond, thus ending his days there.

So ends the story, and it is but a human chronicle. But it is a human chronicle that reflects honor and compassion, broken though it is and marred by human frailty. It is a human chronicle which, though it is a mere shadow of perfection, cannot help but remind us of the real thing.

And what is the real thing? Is it not God's love?

"For God so loved the world, that he gave his only Son, that whoever believes in him should not perish but have eternal life." God's love is infinite and glorious. Planned in eternity, it descended to Bethlehem. It was crucified at Calvary and has conquered death! Yes, this is God's love, and all MacGregor's honor and all Lamond's compassion is invisible next to this love.

Take all of MacGregor's virtues. Take all of Lamond's virtues. Increase them a hundredfold, and you still would not come within an eternity of God's love. He is love itself. MacGregor's love was based on reason: to keep his chieftain's word and to maintain his chieftain's honor. Lamond's love was based on guilt: to pay a debt for a deed hastily committed and rued. But God's reason for love is incomprehensible. It is a deep and abiding love for His children—those created in His image and, though greatly distorted, still the work of His hands. They come from all over the world and God gives them His love freely as a sin offering so that they might not perish but have eternal life.

Beloved, if God so loves you, shouldn't you love one another?

FOOD FOR THOUGHT

1. Explain the last sentence in your own words.
2. In Hosea 6:6 God says: "For I desire steadfast love and not sacrifice, the knowledge of God rather than burnt offerings." What is the difference between doing something out of duty or out of love?

18

HAECKEL'S PRISON

Once upon a time there was a child by the name of Ernst Haeckel. He was born in Germany in 1834. His parents were decent, hard-working people, and they taught their son from the Bible. This teaching included, of course, the concept that it is wrong to lie. While Ernst was young, he did not question the Bible. As he grew older, however, he began to doubt whether God had really created the world. He wondered whether Adam and Eve had been real people, and he asked himself whether God truly existed. Ernst loved nature to such an extent that, in due time, he began to worship nature instead of God. Becoming a field naturalist and zoologist, he used the talent that the God he no longer believed in had given him to draw pictures of the many things he saw outdoors.

In 1866, Ernst Haeckel, who was then thirty-two years old, met a man by the name of Charles Darwin. Darwin had written a book called *The Origin of Species*, a book that Haeckel greatly admired and respected. Haeckel was invited to lunch at Darwin's house, and the two men, although one spoke only German and the other spoke only English, got along very well in broken sentences. It was the beginning of a long friendship.

I write to you, not because you do not know the truth, but because you know it, and because no lie is of the truth. Who is the liar but he who denies that Jesus is the Christ? This is the antichrist, he who denies the Father and the Son. No one who denies the Son has the Father. Whoever confesses the Son has the Father also. 1 John 2:21–23

Haeckel longed for more people to believe what Darwin had written in his book. He wanted everyone to put their faith in Darwin's theory of evolution. The theory of evolution put into words what Haeckel believed in his heart: that all species, the entire plant and animal kingdom, had evolved from natural processes and that God had not really created the world in six days. There was no hard proof for evolution in Darwin's book, so Haeckel thought he would lend Darwin a helping hand. He did this by creating false proof, that is to say, by lying. Haeckel fabricated something that he called a biogenetic law. This law, he said, taught that human embryos exhibited evidence that showed that they had once been animals.

Haeckel then began drawing animal embryos that looked like human embryos. He drew many pictures for the unsuspecting public that "proved" that, in the embryonic stage, animals and people were just about identical. Next to these pictures he wrote things like:

"We see that, at a certain stage, the embryos of man and the ape, the dog and the rabbit, the pig and the sheep, though recognizable as higher vertebrates, cannot be distinguished from each other. . . . This can only be explained by assuming a common parentage. . . . I have illustrated this. . . ."

Wanting to make the theory of evolution true, Haeckel lied through his teeth (or his pencil) with a great many drawings. But the drawings were fairy tales. Embryos of men, apes, dogs, and rabbits are not at all the same. They only looked the same in Haeckel's drawings because he cut off bits here and there and added bits in other spots to make them seem identical.

Lies, however, have a way of coming to light, and Haeckel's fraud came to light at the German university of Jena where he taught. He was charged by five professors and convicted by a university court. His distorted drawings were displayed and called a sin against scientific truthfulness.

The strange part is that many people continued to believe Haeckel even though he was exposed as a liar. Perhaps this was because they did not want to believe the truth. His drawings were, and still are in some places, displayed in textbooks throughout the world. The lie that humans evolved from animals is often still taught.

FOOD FOR THOUGHT

1. The one thing we can learn from Haeckel is that a lie is pushy and rarely gives in to the truth even though there might be much evidence to the contrary. This is because the devil is the father of all lies and he goes about like a roaring lion seeking whom he may devour. Haeckel's lie was part of the devil's great lie. What exactly is the devil's great lie?

2. Haeckel, a first-class liar, and others like him, are in a prison cell of their own making. What is this prison, and what is the door that leads to freedom out of this prison?

19

OF WHOM THE WORLD WAS NOT WORTHY

On July 17, 180 A.D., the courtroom in Carthage was filled to capacity. Those who had not been able to find a seat crowded outside the door, hoping to catch just a glimpse of the proceedings. They were not able to maintain their station long, however. Soldiers pushed them away, clearing a path for the proconsul, who was to be the judge. Spears glittered in the sun. "Move! Move! Make way for Saturnius!"

Although the people were forced to move aside, they did not leave, and a few moments later were rewarded for their tenacity by the sight of those who were about to be tried. A small group of prisoners, chained together, were being herded toward them. Arrested for their faith, six Christians, Speratus, Nartzalus, Citrinus, Donata, Secunda, and Vestia were on their way to court. Some of the bystanders jeered as they passed.

"Away with these traitors!"

But most of the people just stared, rubbing their own wrists in empathy with these young citizens who had apparently broken the law.

Once inside the courtroom, the trial began quietly enough. Saturnius and the other court officials bowed down respectfully to a statue of the emperor. They were acknowledging, to themselves and to the spectators, that they regarded Caesar as Lord. Soberly turning away from the statue, Saturnius faced the six prisoners. His tone, as he began, was gentle and persuasive. "You shall not be punished," he spoke softly, "if you acknowledge Caesar. It is no great matter. Just acknowledge that Caesar is God. One sentence will suffice to set you free."

Speratus answered for the whole group.

"Why, sir, do you speak of punishment? We have not done anything wrong. We have not committed any crimes. We have never wished anyone ill but have turned the other cheek when we were mistreated. We are surely loyal subjects of the emperor."

Saturnius smiled at Speratus and replied cunningly.

"We Romans are a religious people just like you seem to be religious people. Our faith is very simple. We worship gods and we recognize that the emperor is divine. We pray for his health. Surely you can do the same thing? What harm could come of it?"

Again it was Speratus who responded.

"If you will listen to me but for one moment, I will be happy to explain our faith to you. Then you will understand. . . ."

Saturnius interrupted. He was beginning to lose his temper.

"Do you think that you can convert me? Are you mocking my religion? Of course I won't listen to you explain your faith. It would be better if you agreed to worship the emperor."

Speratus lifted his chained hands as he answered.

"It is impossible for us to say that the emperor is God. We serve the God whom no eye has seen and whom no eye can see. We have never stolen. We have paid all our taxes. In these areas we honor the emperor as lord, king over other kings, and emperor over all states."

Speratus's words and meaning were crystal clear. Saturnius understood them and his face tightened with anger. He turned to the other prisoners, clearly hoping that they did not share the same notions.

"Surely," he said to them, and his voice was loud and authoritative, "you do not all hold to these wrong ideas!"

But Speratus would not be ignored and his reply rang out through the courtroom again.

"Wrong ideas are ideas which lead to, for example, murder or false witness. We do not . . ."

Saturnius interrupted, again addressing the others, "Break with the foolishness this man would have you believe."

For the first time one of the other prisoners replied. Citrinus, in the center of the group, spoke. "Sir, it is no foolishness. We can worship no one except our Lord God who is in heaven."

He smiled, and Donata, next to him, added, "Honor is due the emperor because he is the emperor, but worship can only be given to God."

Then Vestia, encouraged by what the others were saying, loudly acclaimed, "I am a Christian." Secunda, also wishing to speak up for her faith, followed with, "I am a Christian too, and what I am, I will remain, God helping me."

Saturnius shook his head in exasperation and turned back to Speratus.

And what more shall I say? For time would fail me to tell of Gideon, Barak, Samson, Jephthah, of David and Samuel and the prophets—who through faith conquered kingdoms, enforced justice, obtained promises, stopped the mouths of lions, quenched the power of fire, escaped the edge of the sword, were made strong out of weakness, became mighty in war, put foreign armies to flight. Women received back their dead by resurrection. Some were tortured, refusing to accept release, so that they might rise again to a better life. Others suffered mocking and flogging, and even chains and imprisonment. Hebrews 11:32–36

"It seems as if you will all remain steadfast in your confessions to be Christian."

Speratus nodded, as did all the prisoners.

"We are Christians."

The courtroom echoed with the words, and the spectators buzzed with excitement.

"Would you not like some time to reconsider? I offer you thirty days to think on the matter. You are young. . . ."

But Saturnius got no further. Speratus and his friends all shook their heads in violent disagreement.

"We are Christians now, and we will be Christians thirty days from now."

It ended the matter. Offended by a loyalty he could not comprehend, Saturnius, the proconsul, finally gave up on them. He asked for a small, waxen writing tablet. Writing their sentence on the tablet with bold, swift strokes, he turned to the court with his verdict.

"Speratus, Nartzalus, Citrinus, Donata, Vestia, and Secunda have professed to be Christians. Although the possibility of returning to the Roman faith was offered to them, they stubbornly refused to accept it. Therefore the verdict is that they be beheaded."

The spectators were amazed at how Speratus responded. "Let us thank God!"

And with feelings akin to awe they listened as Nartzalus also turned to his friends and exclaimed: "Today, fellow martyrs, we shall be in heaven. Praise be to God."

The crowd craned their necks to catch a closer look at the prisoners as they passed by on their way out of the courtroom. Once more being herded together by a small detachment of soldiers, they were chained. Sometimes stumbling at the rapid pace set by their guard, the six passed through the streets of Carthage with a dignity foreign to those watching them. And many people hid their faces from the strength and nobility of their sorrow.

The population of Carthage was only aware of one fact: that the beheadings would take place outside the city gates. They had no idea that the crown of life would also be awarded at that time.

FOOD FOR THOUGHT

1. Hebrews 11:37–38a says, "They were stoned, they were sawn in two, they were killed with the sword. They went about in skins of sheep and goats, destitute, afflicted, mistreated—of whom the world was not worthy. . . ." What does the last phrase, "of whom the world was not worthy," mean?

2. Who is persecuted today? Should your church and family be involved? Why or why not?

20

THE FOUR-DRACHMA
FISHING STORY

There are many avid fishermen and women. Fishing is a sport that seems to enlist fanatics. It attracts people with persevering natures; people who don't mind standing in pouring rain for hours on end holding onto a stick; people who brave blackflies, mosquitoes, and sunstroke just for a tiny tug on their line; and people who can spend hours talking about jigs, rigs, lures, bait, and rods.

There is an amazing fishing story. A man by the name of Blake Robinson was fishing near the Wyoming-Utah border a number of years ago during the ice-fishing season. After various nibbles and bites he finally landed a mackinaw trout—a big one—a keeper. Looking forward to an excellent fish dinner, Mr. Robinson proceeded to fillet the fish. Imagine his consternation when he found a well-preserved thumb inside its belly. It no doubt took away his appetite for a gourmet meal. After asking around, Mr. Robinson was able to return the thumb to its owner, one Bob Lindsey. Mr. Lindsey had been in a boating accident some seven months before and had lost his thumb at that time. Although it was too late to have the digit sewn back on, Mr. Lindsey was happy to have it returned. It was reported that he pickled the thumb and put it in a jar.

March is one of the ice-fishing months in the province of Ontario, Canada. March, by the way, corresponds to the Jewish month of Adar, the time when the towns and villages in Palestine during Jesus' time had to pay their temple tax. Booths were set up in towns and villages and if you missed payment by the 25th of Adar, you had to travel all the way to Jerusalem to pay directly at the temple itself.

So what does this have to do with fishing? Well, there's an amazing fish story in the Bible about tax payment during the month of Adar. Incredible though the story about Mr. Robinson's catch and Mr. Lindsey's thumb is, the story in the Bible has it beat.

Jesus and his disciples had just arrived in Capernaum. Tax booths had been set up in various spots. When Peter passed one of these booths, a tax collector questioned him.

"Doesn't your teacher pay the temple-tax?"

Peter, a fisherman turned disciple, didn't hesitate for a minute.

"Yes, He does."

He knew that Jesus would not break the law.

When Peter approached Jesus for the temple tax payment a little later on, Jesus asked Peter a question in return.

"From whom do kings collect tax, from their sons or from foreigners?"

"From foreigners," Peter replied.

And Jesus went on to say, "Then the sons are free."

Jesus, you see, was the Son of God. The temple was His Father's house, and He did not need to pay tax for its upkeep. Nevertheless, not wishing to appear to set a bad example, Jesus paid the tax, both for Himself and for Peter.

> *While walking by the Sea of Galilee, he saw two brothers, Simon (who is called Peter) and Andrew his brother, casting a net into the sea, for they were fishermen. And he said to them, "Follow me, and I will make you fishers of men." Immediately they left their nets and followed him. And going on from there he saw two other brothers, James the son of Zebedee and John his brother, in the boat with Zebedee their father, mending their nets, and he called them. Immediately they left the boat and their father and followed him.*
> *Matthew 4:18–22*

But He paid it in a most unusual manner. He did not ask Judas for the money bag. His Father's vast resources were at hand.

Jesus told Peter to go to the seaside to fish. The instructions He gave to Peter did not include bait, or lure, or any special technique. The seasoned fisherman was simply told to drop a hook into the sea. And, Jesus told him, the first fish to bite would have a stater in its mouth, that is to say, a four-drachma coin. A double drachma was the tax for one person. The four drachma was the exact change needed to pay both Jesus' and Peter's taxes.

What a marvelous way for Jesus to show that He was God's Son! What a wonderful way to indicate His authority over the sea and its creatures!

More than one hundred years ago, a man by the name of Izaak Walton penned the following verse:

For so our Lord was pleased much, when
He fishers made fishers of men;

Where (which is in no other game)
A man may fish and praise His name.

FOOD FOR THOUGHT

1. Why do you suppose that the experience of finding the four-drachma coin helped Peter, and you, to become less impetuous and more rock-like?

2. Proverbs 11:30 says: "Whoever captures souls is wise" and Daniel 12:3: "And those who are wise shall shine like the brightness of the sky above; and those who turn many to righteousness, like the stars forever and ever." Keeping these two verses in mind, why would you want or not want to be a fisher of men?

21

YOU MUST BE BORN AGAIN

There once were two Jews. The first was a rabbi who had never read the New Testament. The second, a Jewish friend who had become a Christian, spoke to him one evening.

"Please permit me," said the Jewish friend, "to read the New Testament with you."

"Fine," answered the rabbi, "I will have you cured of your Christianity in no time."

They met together and read the New Testament from eight o'clock in the evening until one o'clock in the morning. The rabbi listened with amazement as his friend read to him, every now and then saying:

"Oi, vi shein! Oi, vi shein! Dus hob ich nicht gewist!"

Translated from the Yiddish this meant: "Ah, how beautiful! Ah, how beautiful! I never knew this!"

The rabbi slept at his friend's house that night and on the following morning asked him not to tell anyone in his synagogue that he had read the New Testament. His

> *Nicodemus said to him, "How can a man be born when he is old? Can he enter a second time into his mother's womb and be born?" Jesus answered, "Truly, truly, I say to you, unless one is born of water and the Spirit, he cannot enter the kingdom of God. That which is born of the flesh is flesh, and that which is born of the Spirit is spirit. Do not marvel that I said to you, 'You must be born again.' The wind blows where it wishes, and you hear its sound, but you do not know where it comes from or where it goes. So it is with everyone who is born of the Spirit."*
> *John 3:4–8*

friend agreed but encouraged him to let his congregation know that he thought the New Testament a beautiful book.

But the rabbi, even though he had received the seed of God's word with open ears and even though he thought the New Testament a beautiful story, did not believe it in his heart. Consequently, he bore bad fruit. When his Christian friend visited him again, the rabbi joked about Jesus, reviling His most holy name and laughing at Christianity in front of the students he was teaching. Shortly afterwards, the rabbi was arrested by the Nazis and killed by them in a concentration camp.

The second Jew, the rabbi's friend, had not been brought up to believe in Jesus as His Savior either. Indeed, when he first read the New Testament, he had tried to run away from the teachings of Christ. Even as the rabbi had done, he had initially scorned Jesus. He had mocked Him, continuing in blasphemy for quite some time. But in the end the Man from Galilee overcame him. Richard Wurmbrand, for that was the second Jew's name, was born again. He repented and became a preacher, a preacher of the Good News in Christ Jesus. Imprisoned by Communists, he spent fourteen years in jail for the sake of the gospel. He died in February of 2001 and with his last breath spoke to others about the great love of Christ for sinners.

Even as a chick must hatch, even as a blossom must bud, and even as a river must flow, so those chosen by God must be born again. And having been born again, they cannot help but turn to Him, to acknowledge Him before others, and to live a life that honors Him.

FOOD FOR THOUGHT

1. How do you know that Richard Wurmbrand was born again?
2. Can you make someone else believe? Check out what Jesus says in John 6:65 and comment on it.

22

THE MARRIAGE BOND

Winifred Herbert was the daughter of the English Lord Powys. A beautiful, young girl who was brought up in Britain in the early years of the eighteenth century, she married William Maxwell, the Scottish Earl of Nithsdale. William and Winifred were blessed with a baby girl, and their life together was happy enough until William was convicted of treason in 1715. Together with some other men, he was involved in a Jacobite plot to overthrow George I of England, a plot that would put the Scottish Stuarts in power. William protested at his trial that he had been drawn into the plot against his will, but he was incarcerated nonetheless in the Tower of London and awaited sentencing.

When Winifred heard of her husband's imprisonment, she immediately set out from her Scottish home on the highlands for London. It was December and bitterly cold. Others warned Winifred that she would never reach London during this time of the year. The roads, she was told, would be impassable. But Winifred was not to be stopped. Together with a trusty maid she set off on horseback and by

He answered, "Have you not read that he who created them from the beginning made them male and female, and said, 'Therefore a man shall leave his father and his mother and hold fast to his wife, and they shall become one flesh'? So they are no longer two but one flesh. What therefore God has joined together, let not man separate." Matthew 19:4–6

traveling various routes eventually reached London. It was no easy trip. She later wrote: "The snow was so deep that our horses were in several places almost buried in the snow," and "I must confess that such a journey I believe was scarce ever made, considering the weather, by a woman. . . ." But she was not sorry she had come and added: "However, if I meet my dear lord well, and am so happy to be able to serve him, I shall think all my trouble well repaid."

Winifred was ill the first few weeks she was in London, but as soon as she was well she visited the Tower of London and requested permission to visit her husband. Permission was not granted, but the intrepid Winifred did not give up. She daily loitered on the premises of the Tower and struck up friendships with the guards. They admired her brave demeanor and cheerful disposition and, after a short period of time, relented and permitted her to visit her husband freely. As a matter of fact, they became so used to her constant presence, they stopped questioning her motive for being there.

Winifred did not feel cheerful as she walked through the halls of the prison. The petition she had sent to King George I, pleading for her husband's life, had been denied, and she knew that unless William escaped from the Tower, his death was certain.

Persevering in hope, however, Winifred hatched a plan of escape. She persisted in daily attendance and also told the guards that her petition to the King had been passed in her husband's favor. The guards, who felt sorry for her, were pleased for her sake and even more so when she gave them money to drink to the King's health.

One afternoon Winifred arrived at the Tower with her maid and, as was her custom, walked directly through the corridors to visit her husband. Unbeknown to the guards, she had left her landlady waiting in a coach on the street. Winifred's maid was dressed rather warmly, but no one seemed to notice. As they entered the prison cell, William rose to greet them. The maid immediately began to strip off some of the extra clothing she was wearing, and Winifred piled these garments behind the door. As soon as the maid was done, Winifred took her out of the cell again and walked her to the street. She reentered moments later with the landlady, also dressed rather thickly. The guards laughed as the girls passed, chattering to one another, not really noting that one of them was a different woman. Winifred and her landlady safely entered the prison cell.

Upon entering the cell a second time, the next phase of the plan began. As the landlady took off the extra clothes she had worn for the condemned man, Winifred took a vial of dye out of her skirt pocket and began to lighten her husband's eyebrows. She also had a twist of yellow hair in her pocket and proceeded to fasten tendrils of it in her husband's hair. She then smeared some white paint onto his long, dark beard for she had not the time to shave him clean. No doubt William Maxwell was pleased that his wife should go to such lengths to save him, but he must have felt somewhat foolish as he was obliged to step into layer upon layer of petticoat and satin. But also keenly feeling the presence of the looming axe, he must have born the indignity with fortitude. Winifred fussed and smoothed the skirts billowing over his pants and dabbed some red paint onto his white cheeks. Then she threw a cloak around him and studied the effect.

At this point the landlady left the cell again. Winifred went with her and again made it to the street without any trouble. She then returned to her husband. After a short period of time, she opened the prison door once again. It was dark by now. Winifred counted on the shadows to hide some of her husband's ungainly features as well as on the fact that the guards would hopefully not have counted the times that she had come in and out of the cell with another woman. She walked William down the passage, talking constantly. They made it safely to the courtyard and street, at which point a friend stepped out of the shadows, took hold of William's arm and walked away with him.

Bravely Winifred walked back alone to her husband's chamber in the Tower, later recording, "When I got into my lord's chamber, I spoke to him as if he were there, and I answered as he would answer, and imitated his voice as near as I could and walked up and down the room." After a long time, she went to the door and half-opened it. She put herself in the doorway and turned toward the cell, taking her leave of the empty room as if William were there. After passing into the hall, she closed the door behind her and said to the guards, "I pray you—do not disturb my lord. He is at his prayers." The guards smiled at her and saluted. She passed out into the street safely and breathed a sigh of relief.

William Maxwell was taken to the Venetian ambassador and after a few days of hiding was smuggled to Dover. Through ingenuity, perseverance, and providence, yes, most

of all providence, Lady Winifred Nithsdale had been able to save her husband. She had risked her own neck for him. Hers was an amazing love, for by all historical accounts, Maxwell the Earl of Nithsdale was not a particularly handsome or even clever man, and he is also recorded to have had a disposition for squandering money like water. But Winifred remained, through all his difficult circumstances, a loyal wife and, as such, did her utmost for the man to whom she had pledged her marriage troth before her Maker.

FOOD FOR THOUGHT

1. How is Winifred a godly example to both women and men today in their marriage relationships?
2. Romans 5:8 says: "But God shows his love for us in that while we were still sinners, Christ died for us." If love would only encompass the good, the cheerful, the beautiful, the clever, and the rich, where would that leave you?

23

THE MARSEILLAISE

On April 20, 1792, Louis XVI of France declared war against Austria and Prussia. French troops were immediately called out and volunteers were enrolled in every village and town. As artillery wagons rumbled by and trumpets resounded over roads, excitement reigned. The declaration of war was dutifully read in all town squares throughout the country. Most families, however, were not eager for their husbands and fathers and sons to leave home. Had there not just been a revolution? Had not much blood been shed in that event? Shutters closed, and often people ignored the call to arms.

The mayor of Strasbourg also read the declaration of war. He was a French patriot and eager to have men volunteer. He wanted enthusiasm for the war effort. Knowing that music often got people very excited, the mayor of Strasbourg asked a young captain by the name of Rouget de Lisle to write a patriotic march to inspire people. Rouget agreed.

Rouget was a poet and a composer whose poems were rarely printed and whose songs were rarely performed. Flattered by the mayor's attention, he began work on a march that very evening. Sitting in his small room, he bit the

> *Thus says the LORD: "Let not the wise man boast in his wisdom, let not the mighty man boast in his might, let not the rich man boast in his riches, but let him who boasts boast in this, that he understands and knows me, that I am the LORD who practices steadfast love, justice, and righteousness in the earth. For in these things I delight," declares the LORD.*
> *Jeremiah 9:23–24*

end of his quill thoughtfully. Words resounded in his mind — words from speeches and proclamations. "Aux armes, citoyens! Marchons, enfants de la liberte!" Stimulated by the memory, he wrote the first two lines:

Allons, enfants de la patrie, (March, children of the fatherland)
Le jour de gloire est arrive! (Your hour of glory is here)

Rouget liked those words. He picked up his violin and a melody came to him. It was a wonderful melody, and through the notes he could hear the marching of a thousand feet. Rouget put down his violin and wrote more words, and the melody poured through his veins as he wrote. Before dawn the song was complete and Rouget was exhausted. He sank down on his cot and slept. But the table next to his bed held verses and music, verses and music that would go down in history.

On June 22, 1792, a banquet was given in Marseilles for five hundred young volunteer soldiers. In the middle of the banquet a young man stood up and sang Rouget's song.

None of the volunteers had heard the song before but they were stirred by both the words and the melody. As several stanzas went by and the refrain was repeated again and again, it sparked enthusiasm. Before long five hundred male voices thundered the refrain together. The volunteers took Rouget's song with them to the front. They sang it on marches, through villages and towns, and before long it became known as the marching song of the Marseillaise. It was only a matter of time before all of France was humming, singing, and playing it.

Rouget's name was not printed on the innumerable copies that were being circulated throughout France. Disenchanted with the new government and the revolution, he had been arrested on a charge of treason. As his song resounded on the streets of Paris and elsewhere, Rouget sat in a dank cell awaiting death. By the hand of providence, the prison where he was held was stormed and Rouget was released.

As a free man, Rouget turned bitter. He felt that he had attained some measure of greatness by writing the Marseillaise. The song, however, had a life of its own. Rouget could hear it being sung everywhere, but no one knew or cared that he had written it. Disillusioned, he lived out his days in obscurity. No one was very fond of the captain dropout who had turned into a sour, shifty character. Creditors trailed him. He spent much time in the debtor's prison and never stopped complaining about the hard blow he had suffered at the hands of the government by not receiving credit for a song he had written.

When Napoleon became emperor, he banned the Marseillaise as being too revolutionary. After Napoleon, the Bourbons likewise prohibited the song. In 1830, under Louis Philippe Napoleon, the song was brought back, and Rouget was finally given a small pension for having written it. But he did not enjoy this pension for long. Rouget de Lisle died in 1836, a mean, miserly man who had been interested only in furthering his own interests.

Many years later, long after the Marseillaise had become the French national anthem, the government of France ordered the body of Rouget exhumed. It was reburied near the bones of Napoleon. Would knowing this have made a difference to the little poet-composer so intent on self-glory?

FOOD FOR THOUGHT

1. When it comes right down to it, why should none of our works reflect back on ourselves? When Rouget holds out his composition to God on Judgment Day, what do you suppose God will say?

2. God has created us in His image, and thus He has given us a sense of creativeness. When we draw, sing, sculpt, bake, or write, we use gifts God has given us. What talent has He given you? Explain Ephesians 2:10 which says: "For we are His workmanship, created in Christ Jesus for good works, which God prepared beforehand, that we should walk in them."

24

DAYS OF TROUBLE

Hungry tigers lurked in the mountains. It was quite dangerous to walk about in the foothills alone and unprotected. But the Chinese peasant woman had to feed her livestock, and the foothills boasted much grass. A baby swung on her back in a little cotton hammock, and she held onto the hand of a small child. They laughed and chatted, climbing the foothills slowly. And the woman swung a little sickle in rhythmic motion to their walk.

The grass grew thickly as the foothills rose. The trio stopped walking, and the child sat down as her mother began to cut the grass in a gentle, sweeping motion. But almost as soon as the sickle blade began to cut, a sickening roar turned their heads and stopped their hearts. They had no time to run. A tigress, followed by two cubs, bounded toward them at an angry pace. The child howled and ran to her mother's side. The mother had two things with which to defend herself—a diminutive sickle and a memory.

The Chinese mother did not know how to read or to write. She had never seen a Bible or gone to a church meeting. But a year or two before, a missionary had come to her village. The missionary had been able to plant a seed in this

107

> *Hear my prayer, O Lord; let my cry come to You! Do not hide your face from me in the day of my distress! Incline your ear to me; answer me speedily in the day when I call! Psalm 102:1–2*

woman's heart. This seed was that Jesus can help those who call on Him in distress.

As the tigress leaped into the air, embracing the woman with sharp claws, tearing open her arm and shoulder, the woman cried out in prayer, "Oh, Jesus, help me! Oh, Jesus, help me!" And, amazing as it may seem, the tigress stopped her attack. She turned and ran away, with her cubs following close behind.

Ruth Graham (a daughter of missionaries to China), who recorded this story, does not go on to tell us what happened to the woman. But I think that we may trust that if God answered the woman's prayer this specifically, He certainly went on to help her find out much more about Himself.

Another remarkable story about answered prayer took place in the life of a Dr. Grenfell almost a century ago.

On Easter Sunday in 1908, Dr. Grenfell, who ministered to the sick and injured far up in northern Newfoundland, Canada, received a call to attend an ill man some sixty miles away. He harnessed his huskies and set out. Fog and rain made it hard to travel over soft snow, and Dr. Grenfell, for this reason, guided his sledge over the ice next to the shore. Suddenly the wind dropped, and the gusty power that had been holding the ice against the shore was gone. All around Dr. Grenfell ice was loosening. He could not retreat to safety and was marooned on an ice floe that was crumbling and drifting out to sea.

As night fell, it grew colder. In the rain and fog it was very unlikely that people on the shoreline would spot Dr. Grenfell and his huskies. With a heavy heart, Dr. Grenfell took his knife and killed three of his faithful and beloved dogs. He wrapped himself up in their skins to keep warm and stacked their bodies as a wall against the wind. Then he called for the biggest of the dogs yet living to come and lie down near him for warmth. Dr. Grenfell was a strong Christian, and he fervently prayed to his heavenly Father for strength and relief.

The next morning he was still alive. He continued his vigil of prayer—a vigil that God mercifully answered. Dr. Grenfell had amputated the frozen legs of the dead dogs and managed to fasten them together with a piece of rope. To this he attached his shirt as a makeshift flag. Feebly waving, he was seen the following morning by a boat and rescued.

Neither story proves that whatever you ask God for He will give. It is good to remember Shadrach, Meshach, and Abednego, when they were about to be thrown into the fiery furnace. They acknowledged that God could save them, but they also acknowledged that if this was not God's will, that was still all right. They trusted He would do what was best (Dan. 3:17–18). And so must we.

FOOD FOR THOUGHT

1. We cannot pray if we do not know Jesus. The Chinese woman, even though her knowledge was next to nothing, knew a little. What is the best way to learn about Him?

2. How did you learn to pray? How much time do you spend in prayer and Bible reading compared to spending time talking to friends and reading other books?

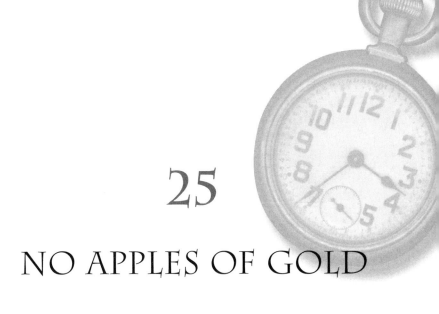

25

NO APPLES OF GOLD

> These apple trees were planted here
> A century ago—
> A hundred years of springtime bloom
> A hundred years of snow.

One of the great legends of American folklore is that of Johnny Appleseed, someone slightly akin in wandering fame to Paul Bunyan. The name brings a picture to mind of a youthful giant—a man with ruddy cheeks, bulging muscles, a cheerful grin, and the physique of a sturdy tree.

The truth is, however, that the legendary Johnny Appleseed was not the carefree, red-cheeked young ecologist he is generally depicted to be. In the early 1800s, John Chapman, later nicknamed Johnny Appleseed, was a very depressed young man. He had been engaged to marry a young woman by the name of Sarah Crawford in a small village church in Massachusetts. Just prior to the wedding, Sarah died. She was buried in her wedding dress with her arms full of apple blossoms, a flower of which she had apparently been very fond.

A word fitly spoken is like apples of gold in a setting of silver. Proverbs 25:11

Perhaps the picture of his dead bride, with her arms full of apple blossoms, gave John Chapman the desire to plant apple trees everywhere. At her funeral, on the steps of the church, he vowed to do just that. He began to travel west from Massachusetts, leaving home and family for an unknown future. Having lost the relationship with the woman he loved, he had no desire for either a permanent residence or material gain. The only things he took with him at the outset of his travels were his Bible and a sack of apple seeds he had laboriously collected from a local cider mill. The poem says:

> The man who planted apple seeds
> Once stood here on this land
> A sack of seeds upon his back
> A Bible in his hand.

As John wandered, his appearance turned rather eccentric. He grew a shaggy black beard, his pants became ragged, and he wore no shoes. The tin saucepan he often wore as a hat also doubled for cooking.

Although at times there were many pioneers on the road with him, John Chapman chose not to settle down. He preferred to wander continually, befriending Indians and planting apple seeds wherever he could.

Apple seeds, though, were not the only things Chapman planted. Well-acquainted with the Bible, he saw himself as a modern John the Baptist, preparing the way, not for

Immanuel, but for the gospel according to one Emanuel Swedenborg (1688-1772).

Swedenborg, a Swedish scientist and mystic, claimed to have been given a special revelation through which he said deep secrets were revealed to him. He maintained that these secrets were the key to understanding the Bible. Although it is a good thing to live simply and in harmony with nature, as Swedenborg suggested, there were basic facts about Jesus that he denied. As such, he was a false teacher. Swedenborg denied original sin, justification by faith, the atoning death of Jesus and His resurrection. John Chapman, alias "Appleseed," passed out Swedenborg tracts with dedication whenever he passed through a town.

In Pennsylvania, Ohio, Michigan, Indiana, Illinois, and Missouri the apple seeds (and tracts) fell into the earth. In 1811, during the battle of Tippecanoe, Chapman could not bring himself to take the side of either the whites or the Indians. In the long run he chose to support both by dragging to safety whatever human being he came across. At one point he was hit by two bullets simultaneously, but strangely unaffected, continued to tend to the injured. At the end of the day, taking his Bible out from under his shirt, he noticed that the two bullets had lodged themselves within its pages.

When he was an old man, Johnny Appleseed did finally settle down in a small cabin in Indiana. It was a cabin surrounded by apple trees. Johnny had shown little interest in material things and had given much love to all living creatures. He gave away seedlings to poor families and his kindness to all creatures from ants to bears to wolves was well known. The Indians respected him, and he was able to come and go freely among them.

For though he walked alone and lorn
Through dangerous land and wild
He said he'd harm no creature born;
Each one was God's own child.

Johnny Appleseed died in his orchard beneath an apple tree after a lifetime of what he deemed to be good works. He had accomplished what he had vowed to do. A monument of apple blossoms declaring his love for Sarah stretched across America. And the God who had created the apple blossoms demanded his soul.

FOOD FOR THOUGHT

1. Why did Johnny Appleseed not have any need of God? Is or is not the epithet "Poor Johnny Appleseed" correct? Why or why not?
2. In Proverbs 3:18 wisdom is called a tree of life and in Proverbs 8:19 her fruit is described as better than fine gold and its yield as surpassing silver. What is wisdom? Comment on the fact that Johnny Appleseed's fruits were "no apples of gold."

26

JEAN MARTEILHE'S STORY

When the Judge smashed down his gavel and intoned the words, "Condemned to the galleys," the prisoner's heart sank. He knew his chances of living a long life had been diminished severely.

An ordinary galley was one hundred and fifty feet long and forty feet wide. The hold of a galley was six feet deep at the sides and seven at the center. The hold was also the place where the rowers sat on fifty rowing benches—twenty-five on each side. These benches were padded with flock wool, or old sacking. Ox hides hung down dividing every six bench spaces into large coffin-like areas—areas into which galley slaves were chained.

A galley slave worked hard. Six men, naked and chained to their bench, together grasped a thirty-foot oar. They had one foot on a heavy bar of wood while the other was braced against a bench in front of them. Their bodies were stretched out, arms stiff as they thrust out their oars overtop of those in the bench in front of them. After they had thrust out the oar, they stood, and the blade of their oar

> *And when you hear of wars and rumors of wars, do not be alarmed. This must take place, but the end is not yet. For nation will rise against nation, and kingdom against kingdom. There will be earthquakes in various places; there will be famines. These are but the beginning of the birth pains. But be on your guard. For they will deliver you over to councils, and you will be beaten in synagogues, and you will stand before governors and kings for my sake, to bear witness before them. And the gospel must first be proclaimed to all nations. Mark 13:7–10*

struck the water. Then they immediately threw themselves down again on the bench behind them pulling the oar toward themselves. If they missed a beat, chaos resulted, and officers lashed out at them with whips.

For food these slaves were given biscuits steeped in cheap wine to prevent them from fainting. As they were rowing, the officer in charge of the slaves put this into their mouths. If one did faint, he was beaten, and if he appeared dead at the end of a flogging, he was thrown overboard. Indeed, the verdict "condemned to the galleys" was nothing less than a death sentence.

It was 1700 and the prisoner, Jean Marteilhe, had been captured at the French border as he was trying to cross over into Holland. The Edict of Nantes, which had given religious liberty to the Huguenots in France, had been revoked, and because Jean was a practicing Huguenot, his life was in danger. He loved the Lord very much and was willing to die for his faith. When the French government condemned him to a lifetime of galley service, he was only seventeen.

Jean served on a French galley for a number of years. He was chained to a bench with four other French men and one Turk. In the seventh year of his servitude, an English frigate attacked his galley. Jean, whose seat was next to the porthole, saw the English ship. The broadsides of the galley and the frigate were so close that by raising himself Jean could reach out and touch the gun pointing straight at the men in his bench. His five companions trembled and lay down flat, but Jean determined to stand up as straight as he could. He leaned forward and lifted up his heart to God. Praying with his eyes wide open, he stared at the gunner as he lit the match to light the gun. The cannon fired and Jean was thrown into the center of the galley as far as his chain would extend.

When Jean regained consciousness, it was night. In the darkness he could see little. He spoke to his five companions.

"Get up lads, the danger is over."

But no one answered. Jean took the Turk by the arm to help him up but shuddered when the arm separated from the body. In terror he let it fall and perceived that all his companions had been killed. Noting then that he himself was bleeding profusely from a wound in the shoulder, the stomach, and the knee, he waited for help as cries of others who had been wounded began to pierce the night around him.

After the French won the battle, men were sent around to unchain the dead and wounded. Jean had fallen into a faint, but when he was unchained he woke and cried out. Perceived to be alive, he was thrown into the bottom of the hold along with other wounded men. The heat was stifling and the stench of putrid flesh unbearable.

Three days after the battle the galley arrived in Dunkirk. The wounded slaves were hauled up with blocks and tackles and taken to a naval hospital where they were chained to their beds. In God's providence a Huguenot friend, who lived in Dunkirk, immediately searched out Jean's whereabouts and found him in the naval hospital. The friend knew the surgeon and commended Jean to his care. The surgeon, who was sympathetic to the Huguenot cause, took Jean under his wing and proceeded to give him the best possible medical treatment. Three quarters of the wounded men died, but after three months, by the grace of God, Jean was pronounced healed. In spite of the fact that he was given a certificate by the surgeon that stated that he was incapable of rowing, Jean was immediately sent back to the galley— and chained to the same bench at which he had almost died.

God continued to watch over Jean and four years later, at the age of twenty-eight, he was released with other Huguenot prisoners as a result of negotiations with the English.

Later that century, between 1746 and 1752, no less than 1,600 Huguenots were sentenced to the galleys. Most did not escape with their lives. Although this was a time period known as The Age of Enlightenment, these white slaves rowed at the command of the "Christian" French king. Many male Huguenots were also hung and their wives were sentenced to prison. Some of these women were young, some were old, some were pregnant, and some were blind. But they experienced a fellowship of saints that only Christians can experience. They nursed one another and cheered each other up. Each year the commander of the prison would write behind each separate name in the prison register, "Sa croyance toujours la meme." Translated that reads, "her faith remains the same." The stories of these saints are legion.

After Jean was released, he sat down and wrote a detailed account of the galleys entitled *The Memoirs of a Man Condemned to the Galleys because of His Protestant Faith.* His memoirs are remarkable because of their detail. They teach us about a number of things—life on a galley, man's inherent evil nature, and the persecution as well as the perseverance of the saints. It was not until 1794 that Napoleon granted complete freedom of religion in France.

FOOD FOR THOUGHT

1. Does North America have freedom of religion? Discuss. Is persecution inevitable for the Christian? Why or why not?

2. When Christ returns, he will find people either sleeping or watching. Which of these two categories fits your community? What can you do to be ready for the Lord's return?

27

NO COALS TO
WARM ANYONE

We celebrate the New Year on January 1. In China, however, the celebration is a bit earlier. In that country the New Year falls on the second new moon after December. Also, whereas in our western culture we celebrate only on New Year's Eve and New Year's Day, the Chinese New Year celebration lasts a whopping fifteen days.

Over the centuries, it has become the custom of many Christians (and that, of course, includes Chinese Christians) to attend a worship service on New Year's Eve. They ponder life's shortness; they bring to mind events of the past year; and they feel very keenly God's purpose and power in the universe. They might sing songs such as:

Hours and days and years and ages
Swift as moving shadows flee;
As we scan life's fleeting pages,
Naught enduring do we see.

The Chinese New Year has also developed certain customs. These customs, however, are not Christian by any means. Incense is burned to relatives who died a long time ago, and these dead people are thanked for their good care. Other idol gods are also prayed to and asked for health, happiness, peace, and prosperity. God, by the way, considers our prayers to Him as pleasing incense (see Rev. 5:8), but He does not think kindly of those who use incense to pray to others beside Himself (see Matt. 4:10).

Because it is considered unlucky to go into the New Year with a bad conscience, Chinese people try to put their lives into some order. They make up quarrels, pay debts, and put their best feet forward. We can possibly compare this to the western custom of making New Year's resolutions.

As was already mentioned, the Chinese New Year celebration is dated according to the lunar calendar, according to the position of the moon. While our calendar has twelve months, the lunar calendar has twelve years. This twelve-year cycle is called the Chinese zodiac.

Each year in the zodiac is named after an animal. The first year is the year of the rat, and eleven other animals follow. They are the ox, tiger, hare, dragon, snake, horse, sheep, monkey, rooster, dog, and pig. Babies born in a particular year are said to have the qualities of that specific animal. In addition to this, the year of your particular animal is supposed to be especially lucky for you.

But is there such a thing as luck? Do the day and year of your birth have anything to do with what will happen to you? Is it right to believe in the zodiac? Even though our North American culture does not have the twelve-year zodiac, it has begun to copy this pagan custom. A twelve-month zodiac is popular with many people and signs such as Virgo,

Stand fast in your enchantments and your many sorceries, with which you have labored from your youth; perhaps you may be able to succeed; perhaps you may inspire terror. You are wearied with your many counsels; let them stand forth and save you, those who divide the heavens, who gaze at the stars, who at the new moons make known what shall come upon you.

Behold, they are like stubble; the fire consumes them; they cannot deliver themselves from the power of the flame. No coal for warming oneself is this, no fire to sit before! Such to you are those with whom you have labored, who have done business with you from your youth; they wander about each in his own direction; there is no one to save you. Isaiah 47:12-15

Libra, and Pisces are household words. There are lots of people (and "Christians" are included) who check out the newspaper to see what their monthly zodiac sign has to say for a particular day.

All major North American newspapers carry a column on astrology. This column can offer very tempting reading material. Who doesn't like to read what might possibly happen to him or her? It affords people a bit of easy guidance and excitement. Little tidbits of advice such as "sharing a delightful secret with that special someone will draw you closer together" and "an excellent day for pushing ahead with business," are actually acted upon by thousands and thousands of people.

God writes a column, too, but it is a column ignored by most people today. He does not mince His words about people who dabble in astrology. In Isaiah 47:13b–15 He mocks astrology and those who listen to predictions. "Let [the astrologers] stand forth and save you, those who divide the heavens, who gaze at the stars, who at the new moons make known what shall come upon you. Behold they are like stubble; the fire consumes them; they cannot deliver themselves from the power of the flame. No coal for warming oneself is this, no fire to sit before!"

Another custom surrounding the Chinese New Year is that of a wicked monster named Nien. Story has it that this monster appeared every New Year to hunt for human food. Fearful of their lives, people stayed inside and locked their doors. Nien was said to be afraid of three things—the color red, the sound of firecrackers, and fire. Consequently, on New Year's Eve people paint their doors red and set off firecrackers. To this day it is custom to hang red and orange scrolls on doorways when a new year is ushered in.

Even though the dragon story is an interesting story, much like a fairy-tale, the superstition it is encased in is very sad. God did not intend for mankind to live by signs and symbols of their own making. As a matter of fact, it is very scary to live by something that we've made up ourselves. It is much better to rely upon the sure promises God has made to us in the Bible. Full of confidence that the old dragon, the devil, has no power over us, we can sing:

Another year is dawning! Dear Father, let it be,
In working or in waiting, another year with Thee;
Another year of leaning upon Thy loving breast,
Another year of trusting, of quiet, happy rest.

FOOD FOR THOUGHT

1. Do you think that habits and traditions not mentioned in the Bible can turn into superstitions? Can they be so strongly enforced that we think our salvation depends on them? Can you mention any?

2. Would it be a good thing to call a New Year's resolution a clean heart resolution? What would such a resolution say about the one making it? Do you know anyone who has made such a resolution (see Ps. 51)?

28

INN OR OUT

Motels are popular. Signs along highways copiously advertise, trying to attract as many people as they can to stay at various inns. Saunas, swimming pools, waterbeds, immaculate rooms, and continental breakfasts, all thrown in for the same price, add up to the plea, "Please choose to sleep here tonight."

Inns have existed for a long time. During the Middle Ages monks constructed low-lying buildings around their monasteries to accommodate the numerous pilgrims visiting shrines. Many of these inns made the monasteries wealthy because pilgrims often brought gifts, in addition to paying handsomely for food and shelter.

When Henry VIII closed the monasteries in England in 1536, inn-keeping turned into private enterprise. The individual rules of owners became the order of the day, and when a traveler came for shelter, he was required to read and abide by regulations such as: four pence a night for bed, six pence with potluck, two pence for horse-keeping, no more than five to sleep in one bed, no boots to be worn in bed, no razor grinders or tinkers taken in, no dogs allowed in the kitchen, and organ grinders must sleep in the wash house.

Many inns in England boast that they have had kings stay with them at one time or another. One such inn, the Ostrich Inn at Colnbrook, Buckinghamshire, dates back to 1106. It is one of the oldest inns in England.

Ostrich Inn is proud of the fact that in 1588 Queen Elizabeth I stayed for an overnight visit. The visit had not been planned. The queen, the story is told, was traveling to London in her royal coach. The roads were not paved (it would be another two hundred years before they were macadamized) and were in a rather sorry state. Potholes and mud puddles were very commonplace. In any case, it was late afternoon when suddenly the queen was jolted off her royal seat onto the royal floor of the royal coach. The floor also dipped alarmingly to the side and she slid against the leather curtain that took the place of a window. Pushing her head out past the leather the queen demanded to know what had happened. A nervous coachman told her that a wheel had come off. He also humbly asked if her majesty was un-harmed.

Elizabeth was not hurt, but her temper was badly frayed. She was tired and disgusted that she would have to wait for the coach to be repaired. The nobles who had ridden along-side the coach informed her majesty that there was an inn, a tolerable inn, nearby. As servants helped the queen down from the coach, others quickly rode to Ostrich Inn to inform the innkeeper and his wife that the queen was on the way.

The bustle that ensued in the otherwise quiet inn was tremendous. The innkeeper's wife put on a clean apron, while instructing her maids to make sure the fire was roaring in one of the guest rooms and that the mattress of goose-feathers in that room be warmed by hot bricks. The cook nervously began basting a beef on the spit while the innkeeper prepared a posset of ale and spices to warm the

> *And Joseph also went up from Galilee, from the town of Nazareth, to Judea, to the city of David, which is called Bethlehem, because he was of the house and lineage of David, to be registered with Mary, his betrothed, who was with child. And while they were there, the time came for her to give birth. And she gave birth to her firstborn son and wrapped him in swaddling cloths and laid him in a manger, because there was no place for them in the inn. Luke 2:4–7*

royal visitor. When Elizabeth appeared in the doorway, everyone curtsied so deeply that they almost fell over. There can have been no doubt in the royal red-headed monarch's mind that she was extremely welcome.

Elizabeth stayed the night, and was quite comfortable. The next morning, her coach being in tip-top shape once again, she left the Ostrich Inn premises feeling rested and relaxed. She rewarded the innkeeper and his wife with gold coins and stated that their inn had been tolerable. But she did add that the state of the Colnbrook roads was rather shocking.

And now, more than four hundred years after the fact, Ostrich Inn uses this royal visit as a drawing tool for tourists. They proudly advertise "Queen Elizabeth slept here." People do come. They want to sleep where this famous monarch slept, eat where she ate, and sit where she sat. Elizabeth has, meanwhile, died. She was an earthly monarch, you see, and subject to mortality.

There is a town in northwest Jordan. Jordan is in the Middle East. It's not a very large town, and about two thousand years ago it also had inns. And the fact of the matter is that when a monarch passed through at that time, albeit in the womb of His mother, no one was anxious to have Him stay at their particular place of lodging.

He was the greatest monarch of all time. His name was, and is, Wonderful Counselor, Mighty God, Everlasting Father, and Prince of Peace.

FOOD FOR THOUGHT

1. The truth is that all our hearts are inns—lodging places for the Prince of Peace. You will know that if you love Him. During the time when we especially remember His birth, a time when so many advertise to have you stay with their particular brand of Christmas festivity, how can you make sure that you advertise proudly and without hesitation that you have Christ living within you?
2. How does your home show hospitality?

29

METATHESIS

Holding small, newborn infant William in her arms, Mrs. Spooner had no idea that this young, squealing baby would someday be a household name—a name that would make people reflect and smile. She cuddled the child tenderly and considered that he was fair, very fair. His silken hair was pure white and his wide-open eyes seemed reddish. His skin also appeared to have an unusual milky hue unlike other babies who were red and pink at birth.

Baby William Spooner, born in England in 1844, grew into a fair-haired child, a rather serious child. Over time the child grew into a young man who felt he had a calling to become a minister. He studied hard and became a pastor in the Anglican Church of England. When he was a bit older, he was appointed dean and warden of New College, Oxford. Although William was a very learned man, he had a peculiarity that caused people to perk up their ears whenever he preached to a congregation or lectured to students in Oxford classes. This peculiarity might have had to do with the fact that he was an albino. He had been born with a congenital absence of pigmentation. That is to say, he had pale, milky skin, light hair, and pink eyes. A nervous person who had poor eyesight, William Spooner continually transposed the letters, syllables, and sounds in a word or sentence. There were times, for example, when he referred to himself as Spilliam Wooner. The scientific name for his speech problem was metathesis.

Long before William Spooner was born, the accidental transposition of letters or syllables in the words of a sentence was already known. Through his lectures and sermons, however, Spooner made the errors so noticeable that the problem became known as Spoonerism. "We all know what it is to have a half-warmed fish inside us," he once told an audience, meaning to say "half-formed wish." William Spooner was a pastor as well as a teacher at Oxford, and many of his slip-ups occurred in church. He once told a lady, "Mardon me padom, this pie is occupued, allow me to sew you to another sheet." Performing a marriage ceremony, he told a jittery bridegroom that it was "kisstomary to cuss the bride."

William Spooner's classes were, obviously, popular. His students listened intently to see whether he would commit some sort of literary blooper. Once he became so angry with a student that he accused him of "hissing my mystery lecture." Another time he dismissed a scholar by saying, "You have deliberately tasted two worms . . . and can leave Oxford by the town drain."

For all his nervousness and poor eyesight, William Spooner lived to be a healthy eighty-six years of age. Some of the best Spoonerisms were coined by others who carefully thought out humorous transpositions of letters and syllables. Spooner himself, however, did leave us a number of delightful phrases such as: "The cat popped on its drawers" (the cat dropped on its paws); "Is the bean dizzy?" (Is the dean busy?); "the assissination of Sassero" (the assassination of

A glad heart makes a cheerful face, but by sorrow of heart the spirit is crushed. Proverbs 15:13

A joyful heart is good medicine, but a crushed spirit dries up the bones. Proverbs 17:22

Cicero); "tons of soil" (He meant farmers here—sons of toil); and "one swell foop" (one fell swoop).

Hundreds and hundreds of Spoonerisms have been attributed to William Spooner. In his sixties, toward the end of the First World War, he patriotically sang out to a gathering of people, "When the boys come back from France, we'll have the hags flung out." He once referred to Queen Victoria as "our queer old dean" (but was not arrested for it), and upon meeting an old friend he amicably said, "I remember your name perfectly, but I just can't think of your face."

There is no doubt that words have to be read and pronounced carefully. Every now and then an error in printing or reading, however, can cause laughter—healthy laughter that is good for the heart. In 1978 a British National newspaper stunned its readers with the headline: "The Pope Dies Again." A Paris newspaper once ran two unrelated paragraphs together: "Dr. F. has been appointed to the position of head physician to the Hospital de la Charite. Orders have been issued to the authorities for the immediate extension of the cemetery at Mont-parnasse."

A slip of the tongue—a slip of the pen—when all is said and done, it is important, as Spooner said, to be spell woken.

FOOD FOR THOUGHT

1. Do you like to laugh? What kind of things do you laugh at? Can you laugh at the wrong things?
2. Is it important for a Christian to be able to laugh heartily and joyfully? Why or why not?

30

STOCKER'S STAND

In January of 1933 Hitler became the chancellor of Germany. The Nazi party had grown from a small minority to a position in control of city councils. Street names were changed to reflect that control. Adolf Boulevards and Hitler Avenues abounded. Armed Nazi guards were stationed in and around public buildings. Swastika flags flew like vultures over railroad stations and alighted on public schools.

Grafath, a small town in the Rhineland region of northwestern Germany, was typical of many small German towns. Everyone knew everyone else in the close-knit community. By no means Nazi oriented, its out-of-the-way unimportance made it difficult for people to take a definite stand against the growing changes more evident in Germany each day. But brownshirts marched the streets here as in other German cities, and their commanding presence warned the locals that resistance to the new chancellor would be met with brutal force. Conformity to the new system was ordered, and on November 12 of 1933 a plebiscite—a public vote—was held to determine whom the people wanted in power.

When the citizens of Grafath arrived at the polling station on the morning of the plebiscite, they immediately noted that voting procedures differed from that of other years. In addition to the usual curtained, voting booths a voting desk had been brought in. People could choose whether or not to cast their votes openly, that is to say in full view of the local Nazi authority, or whether they would hide their votes by entering the curtained booths. Everyone was subdued and no one spoke. A long queue formed in front of the wooden desk. Not one soul in the whole town had the temerity to walk toward a curtained booth.

A bit later on in the morning, however, a gentleman strode into the polling station. He made his way past the queue, took off his hat, nodded to several people waiting in line, and made no bones about the fact that he was heading toward a curtained booth. He was an older man—sixty years old, in fact—and his name was Adolf Stocker. A highly respected businessman of Grafath, Stocker carried himself with dignity, smiling to the silent but gaping crowd as he closed the curtains of the booth behind him. Emerging shortly afterwards, he put his hat back on, gave the Nazi official a baleful glance, and strode out of the station.

At six o'clock the polling stations closed, and by eight it was reported on the radio newscast that Germany had cast an almost unanimous "Hitler vote." In the town of Grafath there had been only one dissenting vote, and everyone in town knew who had cast that vote. Within an hour, a large group of people stirred up by the brownshirts had surrounded Stocker's house. They carried kerosene torches. As this mob closed in on his residence, a raucous voice began to shout into a loudspeaker, asking the same question over and over.

"What should we do with Stocker? What should we do with Stocker?"

The crowd answered as one, heating up as time wore on.

"Aufhangen! Aufhangen!" ("Hang him! Hang him!")

The LORD is my light and my salvation; whom shall I fear? The LORD is the stronghold of my life; of whom shall I be afraid? When evildoers assail me to eat up my flesh, my adversaries and foes, it is they who stumble and fall. Though an army encamp against me, my heart shall not fear; though war arise against me, yet I will be confident. Psalm 27:1-3

Then as suddenly as the disturbance had started, the people disbanded. The whole scenario had been a carefully staged event by the Nazis.

One of the great tragedies of this controlled mob was that Stocker's two sons had been a part of it, shouting alongside the others that their father should be hanged. The Nazis did not hang Adolf Stocker, the only man in Grafath who had stood up to their wicked ideology and rigged election. But the Gestapo did arrest him the following day, and he spent the next six months in prison.

Adolf Stocker was cruelly used by the Nazis as an example of what would happen to those who did not kowtow to their commands, to those who did not cooperate with their point of view. But time is a strange thing! In hindsight Stocker, who was bullied, ill-treated, and imprisoned, is not to be pitied. Rather, he is a glowing example of honor, of living up to principles, and of courage that did not submit or yield to evil.

FOOD FOR THOUGHT

1. "The only thing we have to fear," said United States President Franklin D. Roosevelt in his first inaugural

address in 1933, "is fear itself." Was he right? Prove your answer from the Bible.

2. Paul teaches in 1 Corinthians 16:13, "Be watchful, stand firm in the faith, act like men, be strong." What do you suppose he is telling his readers to watch for?

31

SARAH'S SONG

One evening sometime in the year 1810, certainly a very long time ago, a little five-year-old girl was very upset. Her eyes were red and sore because she had cried for hours. Unable to go to sleep, her hands were clenched into small fists underneath a crumpled wool blanket. Her mother, whom she had loved very much, had died that day. Wee Sarah, for Sarah was her name, burrowed a tired, tear-stained face into the pillow. She was convinced that life could not go on.

But life did go on. And Sarah grew up. She grew up, as a matter of fact, into a lovely, sweet, and talented young lady. She became a wonderful actress. Many people delighted in coming to watch Sarah Flower Adams perform in Shakespearean plays. She had a vivid imagination and was able to make drama come to life. But God had other plans for Sarah.

One day, while rehearsing her lines, Sarah coughed. Then she coughed again and noted with alarm that her white handkerchief had stained red. Immediately she knew that she had contracted the same disease that had been the cause of her mother's death; that she had the same illness with which her sister Eliza was also confined to bed. Tuberculosis was a feared word and one that Sarah had learned to dread.

Sarah's acting days were now over, but God had given her another talent that more than made up for the one she had lost. This talent was writing, and Sarah employed it with all her might. Articles, poems, and hymns flowed from her pen. One morning as Sarah was having her devotions, she read the story of Jacob at Bethel in Genesis 28. She was so impressed by the passage that she wrote a hymn. It was a very beautiful hymn and one we still sing today. It is called "Nearer, My God, to Thee."

Seven years after writing this song, Sarah Flower Adams died. Not many people remember small Sarah who wept so bitterly when her mother died, and not many people remember the young woman whose life held a great many disappointments. Yet many people have remembered her song—a song that expresses Sarah's faith and God's faithfulness—a song that comforts them.

On September 19, 1901, churches in every city in the United States were open. This was strange because it was not Sunday. At a certain time during that day people stopped whatever they were doing—whether they were in a shop, on a street, or on a train. Farmers stopped ploughing in their fields. Workmen stopped machines at their places of business. Some people stood quietly on street corners. Others sang. They sang the hymn "Nearer, My God, to Thee." You see, the President of the United States had died. William McKinley had been assassinated. He had been a Christian man who loved to sing hymns. It had been his custom to invite friends over to the White House every Sunday evening for a service of singing. The hymn he had loved best was "Nearer, My God, to Thee."

Jacob left Beersheba and went toward Haran. And he came to a certain place and stayed there that night, because the sun had set. Taking one of the stones of the place, he put it under his head and lay down in that place to sleep. And he dreamed, and behold, there was a ladder set up on the earth, and the top of it reached to heaven. And behold, the angels of God were ascending and descending on it! And behold, the LORD stood above it and said, "I am the LORD, the God of Abraham your father and the God of Isaac. The land on which you lie I will give to you and to your offspring. Your offspring shall be like the dust of the earth, and you shall spread abroad to the west and to the east and to the north and to the south, and in you and your offspring shall all the families of the earth be blessed. Behold, I am with you and will keep you wherever you go, and will bring you back to this land. For I will not leave you until I have done what I have promised you." Then Jacob awoke from his sleep and said, "Surely the LORD is in this place, and I did not know it." And he was afraid and said, "How awesome is this place! This is none other than the house of God, and this is the gate of heaven." Genesis 28:10–17

When President McKinley was shot, and death was very close, he whispered these words: "Nearer, my God, to Thee. God's will be done." And then he died.

Another story about this hymn took place in 1912. It concerns a huge boat, a luxury liner. Those who had made her thought that she was unsinkable. During its first pleasure cruise that boat, whose name was the Titanic, struck an iceberg. And even though the name *Titanic* means great size, strength, and power, the ship began to sink—and to sink rapidly! The iceberg had gouged a great hole into her side, and the ocean sucked her down quickly. There were not enough lifeboats to save all the passengers. Only six hundred people could be crammed into them, and the remaining fifteen hundred people had to stay on the tilting deck. Everyone was afraid. Many people were panic stricken. Then the band leader struck up a melody. The melody was "Nearer, My God, to Thee." And all the people, the dying people, began to sing. They sang until the freezing waves closed over them.

Many hymns have been written. Many have been changed. But, word for word, line for line, the verses in this hymn have stayed the same.

> Nearer, my God, to Thee,
> Nearer to Thee!
> E'en though it be a cross
> That raises me,
> Still all my song shall be,
> Nearer, my God, to Thee.
> Nearer, my God, to Thee,
> Nearer to Thee!

FOOD FOR THOUGHT

1. Psalm 139:7 says, "Where shall I go from your Spirit? Or where shall I flee from your presence?" What do you think that means?

2. In her hymn, Sarah speaks of a cross raising her nearer to God. Why does God often use seemingly bad experiences to bring us nearer to Him?

Christine Farenhorst, author and poet, is a columnist for *Reformed Perspective*, a contributing writer for *Christian Renewal*, and a reviewer for Christian Schools International. She is the author of *The Great Escape*, *Suffer Annie Spence*, *The Letter Child*, and *Before My Mother's Womb*. Farenhorst has also written a collection of poems and co-authored two church history textbooks for children. She and her husband, Anco, have five children, fourteen grandchildren, a dog, a cat, and ten chickens.

Steven Mitchell has been a professional illustrator and designer for over twenty years. He earned a fine arts degree from Bob Jones University and has worked as a marketing staff artist, agency art director, and freelance artist. He and his wife have five children and two grandchildren.